Making Care Work

Making Care Work

Employed Mothers in the New Childcare Market

Lynet Uttal

Rutgers University Press
New Brunswick, New Jersey, and London

Library of Congress Cataloging-in-Publication Data

Uttal, Lynet, 1959–
Making care work : employed mothers in the new childcare market / Lynet Uttal.
p. cm.
Includes bibliographical references and index.
ISBN 0-8135-3110-1 (cloth : alk. paper) — ISBN 0-8135-3111-X (pbk. : alk. paper)
1. Child care—United States—Decision making. 2. Child care services—United States—Decision making. 3. Working mothers—United States—Interviews. I. Title.

HQ778.63 .U77 2002
362.71'2'0973—dc21

2001058696

British Cataloging-in-Publication data for this book is available from the British Library

Manufactured in the United States of America

To Anne Machung
Who should be sitting where I am.

Contents

Preface and Acknowledgments

Because my own experiences will influence how I interpret other people's experiences, I want to preface this book with a thorough description of my own history of making childcare arrangements. While I conducted the interviews for this book, I was also informally observing families with infants, toddlers, and preschoolers interacting with their childcare providers at the places that I used for my own childcare needs. I have three children (now fourteen, ten, and eight years old), and I am finally starting to leave the childcare system behind as my oldest child is now old enough to care for himself and the two younger ones are school-aged and require only after-school and summer care instead of full-time childcare programs. Over the years, I visited many family childcare homes and childcare centers and conducted numerous individual interviews with in-home providers in order to find care for my own children.

I have navigated my three children through a variety of childcare arrangements in Santa Cruz, California; Memphis, Tennessee; and Madison, Wisconsin. This informal fieldwork began when my first son started going part-time to a nonprofit infant/toddler childcare center in Santa Cruz when he was three months old. My first arrangement was the result of a fellow graduate student telling me to get my name on a waiting list at this center when I was only three months pregnant. Originally, I planned to make arrangements with in-home providers or to swap with other new mothers. When these plans did not work out, I made a last-minute phone call to the center and this turned into a part-time arrangement that lasted three years for my first child and later, another three years for his little brother. Off and on, I combined this arrangement with ten hours of care per week by a teenager during the summer or housemates who worked in exchange for reduced rent. My second son's first childcare arrangement started in our home when he was only eight weeks old. My partner and I hired one of the childcare providers we had met in our older son's infant/toddler center. She came to our home with her own infant for a few months until both of our children entered part-time care at the infant/toddler center.

When my older son grew too old for the infant/toddler center, he spent an unsatisfying three months in a family childcare home that I had carefully selected through the childcare resource and referral switchboard. I quickly moved him back to a mixed-age, nonprofit childcare center for potty-trained preschoolers when I realized his official care provider left the children in the care of an assistant who did not follow her philosophy of care. The assistant, for example, would not allow our son to have his pacifier or diapers, even though we requested both. I chose the center recommended by someone whose judgment I trusted, rather than going with the more popular developmental preschool closer to my home.

When we moved to Memphis, our second son went two days a week to a mothers' day out program at a church for one year, then spent his preschool years and kindergarten at the local university's laboratory preschool.

My partner cared for our third son, who was born in Memphis two weeks before I started my first full-time job as an assistant professor, until he was ten months old; then he also went to a church-based mothers' day out program. The next year, while the oldest was at the elementary school, the two younger children went three-quarter time, from 8 AM to 3:15 PM, Monday through Friday, to mixed-age classrooms in the university preschool. Since the preschool was closed during the summer, my children went to a summer camp program at a church in Memphis, where for the first time I was (amazingly) able to arrange care for all three children in one place.

When we moved to Madison in 1997, we enrolled our youngest son in the four-year-old room of a community nonprofit childcare center. He was the first and only of our three children to go full-time, five days a week, 8 AM to 5:30 PM. Until then, my partner and I had juggled our work and school schedules to create full-time childcare coverage for each of our full-time jobs, having our children in paid nonparental care only part-time. We have never used relative care, for-profit center care, or cooperative care for employment-related childcare needs. Usually, we were juggling more than one arrangement at a time.

When conducting ethnographic interviews, especially about a topic that one has personally experienced, the researcher is a "human-as-instrument" whose own experiences and perspectives become part of the data analyzed. Because the researcher is the primary data-gathering instrument, the researcher utilizes tacit knowledge as well as professional knowledge to understand what is being studied. According to Lincoln and Guba, "tacit knowledge must not only be admitted but is in fact an indispensable part of the research process; it will be influential whether its influence is recognized or not" (1985, 198). Unacknowledged perspectives and experiences can lead to misreading the data or forcing data to conform to the researcher's worldview. In order to avoid this methodological and analytic danger, let me make my biases explicit.

The types of care that I used suggest several biases. First, I did not want my children to be in full-time nonparental care. Second, it also suggests that I did not like what I saw when I visited for-profit centers or interviewed individual in-home providers when I was searching for care. I also was more successful in making childcare arrangements through recommendations from my personal, informal networks than impersonal resource and referral services, even though I ended up in formal, nonprofit, center-based care instead of informal types of care.

With the exception of the one family childcare home, I have not felt that any of my childcare arrangements were damaging to any of my children. Even in the family childcare home, I felt I had an adult I connected with and communicated with about my child's care. The difference was that the person I communicated with was not the person who was actually providing care for my children, and it took me three months to realize that. Like the mothers that you will meet in this book, I became concerned with things that I didn't understand or feel comfortable with. I chose to pay for the kind of care that I wanted. Unlike most of the mothers in this book, I had a job that allowed for great flexibility in my work schedule to address my childcare concerns. I had a partner who was as involved as I was in making and monitoring the arrangements. I had very stable, long-term relationships with childcare providers, using the same childcare provider with subsequent children. When things bothered me, they did not lead to lingering doubts about the quality of care. Because of my own experiences, I did not initially understand what many of the mothers I interviewed were doing. Why did they stay in situations they did not feel comfortable with? Why didn't they just ask about their concerns? Why didn't they have close relationships with their childcare providers? Why didn't their childcare arrangements feel like their community? In order to see their experience, I had to listen carefully to what they said without judging them.

Because I was in the thick of making childcare arrangements myself, it was easy and commonplace for me, as a new mother balancing work and family, to have conversations about nonparental childcare arrangements with other mothers. This was an urgent topic that we talked about, regardless of our own lifestyles, cultural values, socioeconomic locations, or definitions of what counts as quality care. When we worried about our childcare arrangements together, we understood with the greatest sympathy what each other was going through. What was shared across social differences was the understanding that making and maintaining childcare arrangements is a difficult, private responsibility.

Acknowledgments

When I was close to finishing the second draft of this book, I went out to lunch with a group of graduate students to a restaurant where we all had our fortunes read in our Turkish coffee grounds. My fortune told that I was pregnant, about to give birth to something, and that it would be a very difficult birth. Laughing, we all knew that this was a reference to my book manuscript, not an additional child, and, even more confidently, I thought, yes, I have gone through the difficult part already. Little did I know that as hard as it is to write a book, I had no idea how painful it can be to get a book published. Without tremendous support from so many friends and family, I doubt that I would ever have birthed this book. First, it could not have happened without the mothers and childcare providers who were willing to be interviewed and share their experiences. Then there are those who provided child care for my own children over the last fourteen years, giving me the time to think about this topic. To each and every childcare provider, I give big thanks. The development of ideas was assisted by a bunch of great people—especially Linda Roberts and Dan Veroff, and also Shep Zeldin, Gay Eastman, Betty Black, Inge Bretherton, Rima Apple, and Mary Tuominen—who were willing to talk to me about these ideas and read drafts of chapters as they emerged. As my first editor, Grey Osterud was especially important in helping me clarify my points and organize them into a coherent analysis. Willa Speiser also copy edited the text, tweaking words toward greater clarity and rhythm. And to the unknown reviewers who gave great feedback that pushed this analysis into better shape—thanks, even though I don't know who you are (except Naomi Gerstel and Barrie Thorne). I am grateful to my acquiring editor, David Myers, for appreciating the ideas in the book enough to want to see them published.

I am also grateful to those who provided indirect support for my book-writing efforts, first and foremost, my partner, Dan Veroff, for his never-ending support, which came in a million different ways—play that provided relief from working, encouragement and humor when I was in the ditch about this project, and, most importantly, keeping things together at home when I disappeared early in the morning for long hours. I want to give a special thanks to Inge Bretherton, Rima Apple, and my dad, Bill Uttal, for helping me navigate the travails of the publishing market. Thanks to the executive committee of my department, especially Bill Aquilino, who supported and encouraged me. Thanks also, to Janet Hyde, as my U W Women faculty mentor, for keeping me on a strict timeline. I wrote this book while listening to tunes provided by Steve Small—my music companions throughout were Stacey Earle, Kim Richey, Catie Curtis, Lucinda Williams, Aimee Mann, Julie Miller, and Alice Peacock. Thanks to Thomas for head massages.

Financial support has been provided over the years by the University of California, Santa Cruz; Feminist Studies Focused Research Activity grants; University of Wisconsin Graduate School grants; a grant from the University of Wisconsin System Institute for Race and Ethnicity; research start-up funds from the University of Wisconsin, School of Human Ecology; paychecks from the University of Wisconsin, Madison; and sharing a checking account with Dan Veroff.

I also want to say thank you to my children—David, Eli, and Benji—for putting up with the kind of lifestyle that comes with growing up with a mother who is an associate professor. It is their existence that introduced me to the world of child care and made me care to think—even worry—about it deeply. If this book contributes even a little to making the childcare system work better for families, the credit will be due to them. I am glad that my relationship with my guys remains solid—and it's probably at least in part because we had good child care. Last, I want to make a special thank you to my mother, Michiye May Nishimura Uttal, who (though she never read a draft or talked to me about the dilemmas of publishing) provided me with childrearing wisdom and the critical mind to think about the issues in this book.

Love to you all,
Lynet

Making Care Work

Introduction

> The relationship between day care and the family is not then a one-to-one matching of two givens, like one molecule of sodium and one molecule of chloride that put together produce common table salt. It is a rather more complicated chemical reaction. (Steinfels 1973, 221)

The title of this book can be interpreted in two ways, and the double meaning is intentional. This analysis is about both "making care (into paid) work" and "making (paid) care work"—and work well—for the families who use it. The first meaning reflects the commodification of child care and the emergence of a market-based system of childcare services in the United States. The second meaning reflects the daily lived experiences of parents who navigate this system of care and are responsible for ensuring that their childcare arrangement works well for their child.

Echoing Margaret O'Brien Steinfels, Alan Pence and Hillel Goelman note that "a 'best fit' implies consideration of fit at many different points: child, parent, caregiver, neighborhood, community, beliefs, and values. . . . In most families, parents are the ultimate mediator of 'best fit' in day care, yet their voices are strangely silent in the majority of day care studies" (1987, 117). They add, "To better understand day care, these silent partners must be heard" (117). A decade and a half after this recommendation was made, we still do not know much more about how parents view their experiences and navigate their childcare arrangements, what practices make them work, or what practices undermine them.

One of the best ways to understand a common social experience better is to talk directly with those who live the experience. During the 1990s, I formally interviewed employed mothers about their childcare arrangements and had innumerable informal discussions with parents, childcare providers, and childcare advocates about childcare services in the United States.

From my interviews, I learned that each mother creates a special relationship with her childcare provider, regardless of the type of care being used. Each mother brings a unique child, a particular set of family circumstances, and her own assumptions about what child care means. The quality of care in each arrangement is shaped by the interactions of these characteristics with the practices and philosophies of care in a given childcare setting and the values, beliefs, practices, and styles of individual childcare providers. How comfortable mothers were with the mix depended on the relationships they developed with the childcare providers. Their interactions were critical to how well mothers were able to get information about what went on during their child's day and how—or even whether—they communicated their concerns to the care provider.

In 1987, *Time* magazine referred to the childcare dilemma as "the most wrenching personal problem facing millions of American families" (June 22, 1987, 54). Maternal employment was rising, but with only a limited structure of childcare services to meet the growing need for childcare arrangements. The *Time* article cited availability and cost as the two major problems families were coping with. What was most widely available—informal networks of care by family and friends and part-time enrichment programs—was inadequate to fill the demands for full-time child care from the growing numbers of dual-earner and single-parent families. Families were having trouble locating childcare arrangements, facing long waiting lists and no guarantee of care when they needed it.

A later study of childcare costs found that low-income families pay as much as 18 percent of their family income for child care (Casper 1995, 4). Middle-income families pay a smaller proportion of their total family income (7 percent) but still pay large amounts—sometimes as much as it costs to send a child to college for a year—because they pay more for child care than low income families do (Casper 1995, 4). Hiring in-home caregivers is beyond the reach of poor families and an expensive option for working- and middle-class families. Group care in a center or someone else's home has become the more affordable option.

For working- and middle-class families, one of the most dramatic social changes in family and work life was the emergence of a market-based system of childcare services to meet their family needs (Camasso and Roche 1991). During the 1990s, government provided some families living in poverty with childcare subsidies and programs as part of the shift to workfare programs that required welfare families to become working families. An industry of for-profit childcare centers emerged to respond to the growing number of employed mothers. Family childcare homes became more visible as they were transformed from private, informal neighborhood care into more formally organized, licensed small businesses.

The availability of new, market-based childcare services heightens the visibility of childcare options, thus making it easier for working parents to find care for their children. Centers are more visible because they are located in public places, in strip malls or freestanding buildings both in local neighborhoods and in business districts. Childcare services provided by this more formal sector are usually advertised by an agency or company, including listings in telephone books. Resource and referral services also increase their accessibility by making it easier to locate in-home caregivers and other types of independent childcare providers, such as au pairs and nanny services.

As a result of the increasing availability and visibility of market-based childcare services, childcare arrangements have been moving out of the child's home and out of previously established private relationships and social networks. The childcare arrangements used by employed mothers have shifted away from familial and informal ones to more institutional, formally organized ones located in nondomestic settings (Clarke-Stewart 1993). Instead of relatives, housekeepers, in-home caregivers, and neighborhood daycare providers, employed mothers are increasingly taking their children to licensed family childcare homes and childcare centers or hiring the professional certified services of nannies and in-home caregivers whom they may have never met before engaging their services. With the emergence of institutional forms of market-based childcare services, housekeeper care in the child's home has become much less common; by 1990, this type of childcare arrangement represented only 3 percent of all childcare arrangements used by employed mothers (Willer et al. 1991).

The use of childcare centers and family childcare homes more than tripled, from 17 percent of primary arrangements used by full-time employed mothers in 1958 to 61 percent in 1994 (31 percent in another private home, 30 percent in an organized child-care setting) (Kids Count Data Book 1998; Lajewski 1959). The percentage of care provided by nonrelatives almost doubled between 1958 and 1990 from 32 percent to 62 percent for infants, toddlers, and preschoolers with full-time employed mothers (Hofferth et al. 1991; Lajewski 1959). Even private, in-home care has become more formalized as household employees are increasingly obtained through agencies that contract services of au pairs and nannies.

A corresponding decline has occurred in the use of care provided by more familiar others, such as care by relatives or neighbors, and care in familiar settings of friends and relatives. The proportion of childcare arrangements for care of infants, toddlers, and preschool-aged children of employed mothers by relatives both in and outside of the child's home has declined from 42 percent of all childcare arrangements in 1958 to 21 percent in 1990. The only type of relative care that has not declined in the last thirty years is care by fathers (Hofferth et al. 1991; Lajewski 1959).

Families living amidst these changes express a wide range of feelings about how well they are doing with their childcare arrangements. At their best, mothers reflected that their childcare providers "are just like part of our family." They made statements like, "I learned everything I know about parenting from my child's caregiver," or they acknowledged, "I don't know how I would have survived if it had not been for all the support she gave me for being a working parent." When these arrangements are at their worst, mothers expressed serious doubts: "I'm not sure, but I don't think things are quite right, but I don't know what to do"; "I feel like we don't really agree about child rearing, but I don't know how to talk about it with her"; or "I need to find a new childcare arrangement, but I don't have the time and I can't afford anything different than what I have." When these relationships were going well, mothers were comfortable with their childcare arrangements and found themselves worrying less. When they were going badly, mothers reported thinking constantly about their concerns, being filled with anxiety and not being able to focus on their jobs. Making and maintaining arrangements for child care is not a simple process; indeed, it is more like a volatile chemical reaction that may or may not settle down into a stable state of equilibrium.

A Diverse Childcare System

The fundamental reality is that when parents transfer the care of their children to other people, they cannot ever truly know what goes on in their absence. Concerns about safety and physical and emotional care are typical whenever the care of very young children is shifted to others. The emergence of market-based childcare services in combination with existing kin and kith sources of care offer working parents a wide selection of childcare options, in terms of both types of care and cost of care. New kinds of services, such as sick-child care, drop-off care, on-site care, weekend care, overnight care, and second- or third-shift care, continue to be added. Ironically, the ready availability and variety of childcare services through new markets of nonfamily care increases, rather than reduces, parental concerns. The *Time* article's emphasis on matters of affordability and availability implied that the childcare dilemma would be resolved by providing more care at a more affordable cost. It only briefly accounted for concern parents have about the quality of childcare services. The "most wrenching personal problem facing millions of American families" has not been eased by the development of market-based services during the 1990s.

Quality of Care

Having more childcare options does not create more confidence and trust in other people's care for one's child. The difficult problem of ensuring quality care remains to be addressed. It is common knowledge that federal governmental regulations do not adequately set standards to ensure the quality of care, only minimally regulate the staff-to-child ratio and the physical space (such as square footage of childcare centers and family childcare homes), and require only minimal background checks for criminal records and health status of the provider (such as tuberculin skin tests). These token expectations only cover the most basic custodial components of childcare quality. Training and continuing education in child development are seldom required for licensing or employment.

The best definitions of quality include standards for the child's safety, communication between the provider and parents about the child, and a warm and attentive relationship between the provider and child. According to the National Association for the Education of Young Children (NAEYC), high-quality care provides programs that involve children in play and other activities; sufficient staffing to support early childhood development and education; developmentally appropriate expectations; opportunities for physical, emotional, social, and cognitive development; staff who regularly plan and evaluate their program; and close communication between parents and staff (National Association for the Education of Young Children 2001). Additionally, Zero to Three, the National Center for Infants, Toddlers and Families, emphasizes that for younger children, "the key to quality care is the quality of relationships—relationships between the infant and her family, between child and caregiver, between caregiver and family, and among adults in the childcare setting" (Fenichel, Griffin, and Lurie-Hurvitz 1998). Some states and cities voluntarily adopt these guidelines, but federal governmental regulations do not require them. As a result, guidelines vary tremendously from one state to the next.

When I interviewed employed mothers about their childcare arrangements, I heard voices that were full of angst, anxiety, and worries about both current and past arrangements. I learned that finding care and paying for it were only a small part of their concern. They seemed more frustrated than satisfied with their childcare arrangements. Every conversation I had revealed that these mothers constantly struggled with worries about their childcare arrangements. Even when mothers said that they had made careful choices, claimed that their arrangements were the best, and described their childcare providers as close to sainthood, they still expressed doubt—the "are they really . . . ?" and "what if . . . ?" doubts that parents, especially mothers, typically have about childcare arrangements. Their anxiety and ambivalence centered on how to monitor and ensure the quality of their arrangements. Their concerns about the quality of the care included not only worries about physical safety, programming, and staffing but also concerns about the relationship between their child and the childcare provider and what kind of care was being given to their child. Mothers revealed that they worried about many little things that in isolation seemed not so important but taken together or over time raised questions about the quality of care and required their attention. Worries emerged from fleeting observations—for example, that a childcare provider did not respond immediately or compassionately to a crying child, or from discovering differences in styles of care—for example, that the childcare provider used little slaps on the hand to discipline their children. These worries did not reflect apprehensiveness about finding care, affording care, or being a family without a stay-at-home parent, but rather parents' uncertainty about how to ensure the quality of care when they left their children with others.

Parental concerns about substitute care are amplified when families move from care by family members and friends into market-based childcare services because childcare centers and family childcare homes are often staffed by people who are previously strangers to families. These relationships are established initially on principles of exchanging wages for services rather than on principles of care and commitment. Even in well-established, center-based care, high staff turnover introduces another element of instability. Even after familiarity is developed, providers may unexpectedly disappear or leave on short notice. Going outside of familiar kin and kith circles to use market-based care outside the child's home with a continually changing cast of caregivers taps into parental fears about child neglect. Can hired childcare providers provide the kind of loving care that young children need during those long hours of care?

Parents have good reason to doubt the quality of care, especially in childcare centers and family childcare homes. In 1995, one study of centers and family childcare homes found that only 14 percent of childcare centers and 13 percent of family childcare homes achieved ratings of at least good quality (Bryant et al. 1995). Only 8 percent of infant classrooms and 24 percent of preschool classrooms were of good or excellent quality. And 10 percent of preschool programs and 40 percent of infant programs were rated so poor in quality that they jeopardized children's health, safety, and development. Another study found family childcare homes lacking in quality

(Galinsky et al. 1994). Only 9 percent of the family childcare homes studied were found to be of good quality, whereas 56 percent of the homes were found to lack care that would contribute to a positive developmental environment and positive outcomes for children.

Parental fears are also fueled by sensationalist stories newspapers write about childcare arrangements: *A child was sexually abused by a family childcare provider's husband. An infant was shaken to death by a stressed-out, inexperienced au pair. Children were found warehoused with one childcare worker alone with twenty infants.* These news stories exacerbate the doubts and fears parents already have, even without sexual abuse or neglect in their own arrangements.

No matter how carefully parents choose their childcare arrangements, inevitably they will develop doubts about that care. Rather than providing a system that makes it easier for women to enter the labor force and for families to entrust the care of their children to others, the use of market-based childcare services creates a new host of problems. Mothers are worrying about matters that define a broader notion of "quality of care" than the one policymakers and early childhood researchers and specialists usually focus on.

Even though the current childcare system leaves so much up to the parents, childcare researchers do not really know what parents think about their childcare arrangements. This book examines the relationships that employed mothers establish with the childcare providers with whom they share the care of their children, rather than focusing on supply and demand for services or on child developmental issues. By illuminating the issues that concern employed mothers when they share the care of young children with childcare providers, I hope that this book will offer proactive ideas for how families and childcare providers can cooperatively share the care of young children as well as overcome the stumbling blocks. By knowing more about how mothers experience the daily matters of their childcare arrangement, I explain why survey research findings repeatedly document high levels of global satisfaction with childcare arrangements even though mothers worry so much about those arrangements in their in-depth interviews. Despite the uniqueness of each family's experience and their relationship with their childcare provider, there are some common issues, general concerns, and patterns. It is my hope that revealing them will lead to an understanding of what to expect and different ways to handle these inevitable concerns, and will contribute to a broader understanding of the childcare experience and ease the difficulties of making individual childcare arrangements for each family.

Let me begin with examples of three women I interviewed that illustrate the different types of concerns that mothers are coping with.

Brenda Sharpe

"How do I know if they are being as careful as they should be?" Brenda Sharpe, a White, thirty-one-year-old mother, asks about her childcare providers doubtfully. She is worried about whether the childcare workers at her childcare center are paying enough attention to her child, but she doesn't know how to ask them about her concerns. Nine months ago her corporate job relocated her to Memphis, Tennessee, and has kept her working hard, and many hours. She feels lucky that she was able to so quickly find a childcare center close to her home and open long enough hours to accommodate the regular overtime her new job demands. Before she moved to Memphis, her nineteen-month-old son had been in the care of his aunt, a stay-at-home mother with two young children of her own. Although this is not Brenda's first childcare arrangement, it is her first arrangement in the formal market of childcare services, and she is not quite sure what it is reasonable to expect from her childcare providers or how she should communicate with them. When she gets the courage to ask the childcare providers about how things are going for her child or inquire about a scratch on his face, she is dismayed to find out that the providers who are working when she picks up her child do not seem to know much about what has occurred earlier in the day. Many different people are providing care for her child during the course of the day. Brenda isn't sure if she is expecting too much to want her child to receive more individualized attention in a group care setting or to be watched more closely so that he does not come home with bites and scratches. Brenda wonders if she should look for a better childcare arrangement, but truthfully, she and her husband like the convenience of her center, and she does not feel she has the time to go look at centers again, nor does she believe that she will necessarily find something better or providers with whom she will be more comfortable.

Brenda's story reveals that mothers think about the quality of care more broadly than just in terms of providing their children with cognitive, social, and academic opportunities. Their comfort also depends on their understanding of what they can expect from care arrangements and knowing how to ask for the kind of care they want their child to have.

Although some concerns are exacerbated when mothers are novices in the childcare system, this is not a problem that only new users experience. Even when mothers chose carefully and initially experienced satisfaction with their choice, they would inevitably experience doubts, fears, and worries about their childcare arrangements.

Aurora Garcia

"How am I going to tell her that I don't trust her right now?" asks Aurora Garcia, a thirty-nine-year-old Mexican American city administrator, about the family childcare provider who has become like "one of the family," caring for Aurora's three-year-old-daughter since her birth. When Aurora first needed care, she did not have any relatives living near her in Santa Cruz, California. She found Linda Nunez, who ran a Latino family childcare home that Aurora felt replicated the kind of care her own family would have given. Until recently, she has always felt Linda was a godsend to her. Lately, insidious fears that Linda is being less attentive to her child have Aurora worried. Aurora has noticed that Linda seems more distressed about her own family problems with her teenagers, and more and more she and Aurora talk about those problems instead of how Aurora's child's day went. Linda seems to be edgy and short-tempered with the children and the parents, which is unusual for her. Aurora is also newly concerned that the care is no longer developmentally appropriate. For example, Linda may not be reading out loud enough, an activity that Aurora did not consider when she selected her provider for infant care but now feels is increasingly important given that her child is three years old.

Although Aurora is a competent, in-charge kind of person who regularly supervises seventy employees in a high-powered job, she dissolved into hopeless tears as she described how hard it was for her to figure out how to approach her childcare provider with her concerns. She is not sure if her concerns are valid. She wants to continue to trust Linda, but what she observes and from the stories she hears from other parents with children there increasingly make her doubt the quality of care. And to confuse matters even more, she also feels disloyal. She knows that her daughter and her childcare provider have a special relationship with one another. The knowledge of her provider's genuine attachment and care partially overrides her concern about whether the care is developmentally appropriate or not. This prevents her from changing her childcare arrangements just to find more developmental opportunities. She also acknowledges that Linda has been important to her own learning about how to parent. Tormented by her mixed feelings of concern and gratitude, she is trying to figure out whether she should talk with her childcare provider about her concerns, or leave this arrangement for a new one. None of her individual worries seem concrete enough or definite enough to justify confrontation or change, yet she spends hours worrying about the quality of care her child is getting. She is also afraid to tell her childcare provider that she is thinking about leaving, so more and more often she sends her partner in to pick up her child so she doesn't have to face Linda.

Aurora's story reveals that she could not have anticipated either the changing developmental needs of her child or the changing circumstances that would affect the quality of her provider's care. When children spend many hours in nonparental care, mothers also become aware that the extensive and intimate involvement of childcare providers in the lives of children extends to their families, making the relationship between the childcare provider and the child's mother critical. Because of the long hours that very young children spend in care, mothers pay attention to several types of relationships. First, they consider the nature of the social and emotional relationships between their child and childcare providers. They recognize that childcare providers become an important part of their child's life. They also wonder how having others regularly caring for their children for such long hours affects their own relationships with their children. And, finally, mothers also have concerns about the relationships they themselves, as adults, establish with their childcare providers.

Their concerns are not just interpersonal, however. Mothers are also aware that the conditions within which childcare providers work shape their satisfaction with the quality of the childcare arrangement. This is what the mother in the next example worried about.

Gwendolyn Jackson

Gwendolyn Jackson is a thirty-five-year-old African American mother of an eighteen-month-old daughter. She has already used an in-home childcare provider and two different childcare centers in Memphis, Tennessee, since she went back to work when her daughter was four weeks old. Gwendolyn easily establishes good relationships with her childcare providers, making the time to learn about their lives and check on their well-being just as much as she does about her child's. When Gwendolyn came home one day to find her infant alone in a crib in the living room, she worried that her childcare provider, a young African American woman, was too distracted by her own personal problems to provide good care. Even though she liked her very much and wanted to support her, Gwendolyn decided to switch from in-home care to center-based care, where a group of caregivers instead of a lone woman would care for her child. When the childcare center serving African American families from a mix of class backgrounds was regularly understaffed because it could not afford to pay the workers, Gwendolyn worried about whether the underfinanced childcare center could provide adequate care, and she found a center that served middle-class families of different races and was more fiscally able to ensure stable staffing. She regretted that each change moved her one more step away from an African American community, but each step also gave her greater peace of mind. In each setting, Gwendolyn spent a lot of time being involved, providing support to her childcare providers, and making the effort to improve the working conditions by asking the center director to address her concerns about the quality of care and the environment. She tries to make the care better not only for her child but for all the children there. Gwendolyn is concerned about her childcare providers' well-being and their working environment because she thinks these conditions will influence the quality of care her child receives. Sometimes Gwendolyn is able to approach the childcare center director or the childcare provider confidently and check things out, but at other times, she is afraid that if she is too demanding, she will be viewed negatively and her child will be treated less well. Her ambivalence about how to handle her concerns sometimes makes it easier to seek out new arrangements, hoping for something better, than it is to stay put and work with her current arrangement to improve it. Her income, combined with her husband's, allows her to choose care without worrying about the cost, but she is tired of looking for new arrangements, changing her child's care, addressing new concerns, and adjusting herself to the personalities of new childcare providers.

What Gwendolyn's experience illustrates are the multiple standpoints that need to be taken into account in a childcare setting. Childcare arrangements are not just about the child's experience in care but are also shaped by how the childcare provider is doing and whether the organization of the care also supports the childcare worker.

Brenda's inexperience and not knowing what is reasonable to expect, Aurora's changing expectations, and Gwendolyn's search for better arrangements each reflect how volatile childcare arrangements can be. It is difficult to maintain stable childcare arrangements. Brenda is a novice in the childcare system, still learning how to navigate it. Aurora is experiencing the kinds of doubts that emerge because of changes in her child's needs as well as changes in her provider's personal life, and not because of her own inexperience in the use of childcare services. Like Aurora, Gwendolyn is worrying about her providers' ability to provide quality care, but understands that the efforts of childcare providers are tied to and often limited by the conditions under which they work.

Collectively, these three women capture what I heard most often from the women I interviewed. They expressed the common array of doubts that mothers have about their childcare arrangements. Enough love? Is love enough? Are these concerns real enough or serious enough to warrant attention or change? How to balance the child's needs, the provider's needs, the parents' needs? Is the provider in good enough mental health to do the work? Are the working conditions supporting quality care? Is there anything better out there? Whether in new arrangements or long-standing ones, with mothers who can communicate with their childcare providers or not, these are the kinds of doubts that mothers wrestled with.

These mothers' doubts were shared by many of the other mothers I interviewed. The overarching problem was the emergence of concerns about minor aspects of the care and deciding how to handle them. Many of the women I spoke with were struggling to learn the informal rules of their childcare arrangement, as well as how to communicate with their childcare providers about their emerging concerns. Many of them also shared fears about the consequences of raising concerns, wondering if changing arrangements would be easier than directly addressing their concerns. At the same time, they felt they did not have the time and they dreaded the thought of having to initiate a search for new childcare arrangements. Most of them did not believe that they would necessarily be successful in resolving their concerns if they went back "out there" into the childcare market looking for something better.

How I Studied This Social Experience

Using data from individual interviews, combined with information about the political economy of the 1990s and the history of childcare policy in the United States, I sought to understand what was going on. Although individual voices are heard here, the analysis is a collective and societal one, emphasizing common issues and themes rather than particularized experiences or individual trajectories.

These troubled experiences do not happen in isolation. We need to look at both the personal experience and the context in which it is embedded to understand the childcare system today. Individual personal experiences are always embedded in a political economy and ideological system. In this case, we are examining the political economy of child care at the end of the twentieth century, as well as changing gender and family ideologies and how individuals negotiate and navigate them. These systems do not just impose themselves on people; rather, they create a context within which personal experiences are constructed.

My sample of forty-eight employed mothers (see appendix) came from a larger study of sixty-one employed mothers and twenty-four childcare providers that I conducted in-depth interviews with during the 1990s. Although there is a wide variety of ways for parents to secure nonparental care, I have limited this analysis to the subpopulation that exchanges money for childcare services in order to highlight the recent emergence of a commercialized, for-profit market of childcare services. Limiting the focus to families with children who are not yet old enough to go to school captures what happens when childcare services are procured privately by parents without a clear, publicly supported childcare system (such as public school system or statewide four-year-old program) to provide or support their childcare needs. Not included in this analysis are other mothers who covered their employment-related childcare needs by working different shifts than their partners, participated in parent cooperatives, or received free or subsidized child care. Although some of the mothers I interviewed had relatives care for their children part-time, none of them entirely covered their needs with free care by relatives. Even the two mothers who received some free care by relatives combined this with some form of paid care or paid relatives for their care.

What characterizes this subgroup of employed mothers is that they had a range of childcare options. They could afford child care even though they complained about cost, and they were generally comfortable with the idea of having people other than family members take care of their children and using institutional and group settings. At first glance, they did not seem like mothers who would be worried about their childcare arrangements. They were not very poor mothers whose options were constrained by their economic circumstances, nor were their choices limited by their dependence on subsidized care. Many of them had jobs that allowed them a certain degree of flexibility to attend to their parenting responsibilities, and no one was suggesting to them that mothers should not be employed. They were not consumed with guilt about the legitimacy of their employment; in fact, most of them just assumed that combining motherhood and employment was the "normal" thing to do, and they felt comfortable abstractly with the idea of others caring for their children. They had come into motherhood at a time when the cultural milieu supported what Denise Segura has referred to as "nonambivalent employed motherhood," in which "employment and motherhood seem compatible social dynamics irrespective of the age of the children" (1994, 217). Not only were most of their peers employed mothers, but there were also many structural supports for their employment—including the ready availability of a market of childcare services.

The mothers featured in this book are diverse. Twenty-nine of the mothers were interviewed in 1990–93 in Santa Cruz County, California, the other nineteen during 1996–97 in Memphis, Tennessee. Each used care that the family was paying for. I deliberately diversified the sample by race and ethnicity and interviewed twenty-seven White mothers, thirteen African American mothers, seven Mexican American mothers, and one Guamanian American mother. I use a wide variety of labels in the text to refer to these women, depending upon which region of the country they were interviewed in and how they referred to themselves. The reader will also notice that I purposefully omit racial and ethnic identification when they are not relevant to the matter being discussed.

The women I interviewed were purposively selected to represent a range of occupations, including professional, mid-level management, administrative, clerical, and manufacturing workers. Ten were doctors, lawyers, professors, or presidents and vice presidents of companies (professionals/ executives). Eighteen were teachers, nurses, or managers, and in positions that have mid-level professional or administrative responsibilities (upper middle level professional/management jobs). Fourteen were self-employed, worked in labs, or were administrative assistants or managers for businesses and nonprofit organizations (lower middle level jobs). Six worked in warehouses or did clerical or service work (entry-level jobs). I made sure that I interviewed women of color in professional occupations, as well as White women in entry-level positions, in order to avoid a bimodal sample composed of professional White women and working-class women of color. Since previous research has been mostly about women in dual career couples and two-parent families, I also included eleven single mothers (divorced and never married) and eight women living in nonmarital partnerships, including four lesbian mothers. Twenty-nine of the mothers were married.

It is difficult to classify women by the type of childcare arrangement they use because many of them had multiple arrangements. For example, one mother hired five different women who came into her home and watched her child while she worked full-time. Another mother sent her child to a childcare center in the morning and had the child's grandmother care for her in the afternoon. One mother had two children, both cared for in the same family childcare home. Another mother had two children cared for in two different childcare centers. One mother hired her housekeeper to watch her youngest child but relied on a preschool program with extended care for her older child, and had another school-aged child in an after-school program. When women worked evening, weekend, or changing shifts, they often used a secondary arrangement. This variety is often the result of having more than one child, but it is also common for mothers to have multiple arrangements for a single child. Twenty-one of the mothers in this study—

almost half—were managing multiple arrangements for their infants, toddlers, and preschoolers. Seventeen also had care arrangements for school-aged children.

For their primary arrangements, about half of the mothers I interviewed used childcare centers. Of these twenty-six mothers, twenty used childcare centers exclusively, while the other six combined it with other types of secondary care. Thirteen of the mothers I interviewed used family childcare homes; eleven of them used only this one type of care, while two combined it with care by the other parent. One-fifth of them hired an adult (nonrelatives and relatives) to provide one-on-one care in the child's home (eight) or the caregiver's home (one). One mother combined two part-time arrangements with relatives, one paid and one unpaid. Despite this variety of arrangements, mothers expressed common concerns across different types of care.

The purpose of this diversity is to understand the general process of making and maintaining childcare arrangements, rather than presenting case studies of individual experiences or issues specific to one type of care. This study focuses on how mothers feel about whatever childcare arrangements they are using or have used in the past.

The reader will notice that I use direct quotes from some of the same mothers frequently, and others not at all. I elected to use the words of mothers who best represented the viewpoint or issue being presented. Some mothers were particularly articulate about their experiences, so we hear more often from them. The experiences and voices of those mothers who are not directly quoted are nonetheless represented in the analysis, because they share the views that are expressed here.

Because mothers' stories about how they made and changed their childcare arrangements are so complicated, the analysis often weaves back and forth and backsteps across time in the mothers' narratives, so that the same mother may be described at one point as using a family childcare home and at another point as using a childcare center; or at one point a mother may sound satisfied with her arrangements and at another point extremely dissatisfied. This multiplicity in presentation captures the reality of the chaotic, changing, and complicated pathways of childcare arrangements. Individual stories were very complicated because mothers often had used many different arrangements between the time they first began using nonparental child care and the time I interviewed them. They often talked about all of their different arrangements throughout the interview.

The interviews with the mothers began with the open-ended question, "Tell me about the history of your childcare arrangements," and mothers were given the opportunity to talk about what mattered to them. They most often chose to tell me about how they felt about having others take care of their children, what kinds of difficulties they had with working with childcare providers, how much they loved their childcare providers, and how difficult these interpersonal relationships were. Mothers expressed their frustration at being responsible for childcare arrangements in a society that makes child care a private responsibility of individual families and does not value the kind of work that childcare providers are doing.

Several of the mothers suggested that I should also talk with their childcare providers, which I did. If they did not suggest it, I asked them if I could. The mothers' views were complemented by in-depth interviews with nineteen of their paid childcare providers. Six of these childcare providers worked privately in the child's home, one worked privately in her own home with only one child, eight were family childcare providers, and four were childcare center employees. I interviewed childcare providers as deeply as I did the mothers, beginning their interviews with the question, "Tell me how you came to be a childcare provider," and asking them about their relationship with the mother whom I had already interviewed. However, I did not interview as many providers as mothers, and the perspective presented in this book is that of the employed mother.

The analysis is driven by what the mothers wanted to talk about and what I, the researcher, needed to understand in order to develop a coherent understanding of their collective experiences. The focus of my analysis was often generated by trying to understand a contradiction that I heard in their words, both as individuals and collectively. For example, why did all of them (except one) report that they were satisfied with their current childcare arrangements on a satisfaction survey I gave them, yet during the in-depth interviews express so many concerns and worries? Why were so many of them afraid to talk to their childcare providers even though they had legitimate concerns? And, even though they have trouble communicating with their childcare providers, why were they at the same time highly attached to and appreciative of them? Finally, why were they hesitant to look for something better and find new arrangements? These initial questions motivated the development of the final analysis that is presented here.

A Caveat about the Assumption of Mothering

Readers will notice that the language I use is flavored with the assumption of mothering—that is, that mothers are the primary persons looking out for their children's well-being. Even though in this book *child care* means "the social and psychological acts that are done [for their child] by the primary caretaker, regardless of the gender of the person doing them" (Ehrensaft 1987, 9), I did not interview fathers about their views of childcare arrangements. At the time I started this research, my original focus was on how employed mothers used their childcare arrangements to balance work and family. I made the decision to limit my analysis to employed mothers and paid childcare providers because the overwhelming sociological reality was then and still is that women hold the primary responsibility for the well-being of children in paid childcare arrangements.

Many scholars and activists are still trying to figure out why gendered divisions of caregiving persist and how to get men (as a group) more involved in caring, family work, and sharing the responsibility for their children's well-being. In spite of the attention that is being paid to father's involvement in childrearing (mostly at home), and though it has become common to see representations of individual men who have broken out of the traditional mold of masculinity, U.S. society is still structurally and socially organized around the gendered division of caregiving. Women care for children, both as mothers and paid workers. Men who care for children do so as unique individuals, not as products of their gendered social location. In fact, these men are still going against the current norms. Although many different kinds of explanations have been proposed for their low involvement in child rearing and child care—biological, structural, ideological, socialization, rational choice model—the persistence of this pattern is one of the unfinished discussions of our time.

Individual men can and do take on this responsibility and carry out maternal care, regardless of the general sociological reality. So I hope that readers, especially those who are familiar with wonderful men who are sharing parenting or care work as childcare providers, will read this maternally biased text as including them. Readers might ask themselves as they read which of the ideas in this book are transferable to fathers or male childcare workers. Readers might want to refer to work by scholars such as Preston Britner, Jay Fagan, and Susan Murray, who have begun to study fathers' involvement in childcare arrangements and male childcare workers.

Mixing Care and Market Principles

Underlying parental doubts about their childcare arrangements is skepticism that caring relationships can be turned into services or should be bought in a market system. Exchanging money for child care is distasteful because market exchange relationships seem inconsistent with caring relationships. How can child rearing be turned into a market-based service? Can anyone ever be paid enough to care for a child as a parent would, especially a mother? Mixing the market and mothering feels like trying to mix oil and water; a natural drift toward separation seems the reasonable result, no matter how hard the two are shaken together. In fact, trying to mix mothering and the market feels like a violation of an important moral principle about the way the world should be, because today we allow the market to be uncaring and cut-throat, organized around principles of individual profit and short-term gain, instead of collective well-being, commitment, and long-term development of human potential.

When what is normally thought of as a caregiving relationship is transformed into a relationship based on the exchange of wages for services, ambiguity and confusion result (Uttal and Tuominen 1999). In fact, market-based childcare services are premised simultaneously on the rules of the marketplace ("I am hiring an employee to take care of my child") and on the principles of emotional connections ("The person who cares for my children will love them"). Parents often express a desire for family-like care or for the childcare provider to care for their child "the way a mother would." The recent emergence of market-based childcare services raises new questions. How much can parents expect family-like relationships from a market-based service? How do parents feel about having others, especially people who are initially strangers, taking care of their children? And, most importantly, how do they handle the responsibility to ensure the quality of care when the children are spending long hours in nonparental care?

These questions are not unique to child care. Other types of commodified caregiving, such as nursing and elder care, evoke similar concerns. When caregiving is transferred to a paid caregiver, the labor of the physical and emotional work is separated from the executive responsibility for ensuring the overall well-being of the care recipient. The actual provider of the daily, minute-by-minute care is often the person who has the least long-term responsibility for the care recipient. The contractual relationship between the paid caregiver and the care recipient is presumed to be short-term and limited, with money as the sole form of compensation for the care worker. Even if the care worker develops genuine caring connections for the care recipient, maintaining this connection is bounded by the decisions of the person from whom the care has been transferred (for example, the mother, the adult child, the spouse). The manager of the care who controls the long-term decisions about care arrangements may in fact be less well informed about the daily needs of the care recipient than the actual caregiver is (Fisher and Tronto 1990).

A few studies have examined the structural relationship between mothers and childcare providers, revealing practices regarding the division of "mother-work" between the caregiver and the mother and the tendency of parents to expect more from providers than they formally contract for. The organization of paid childcare work can take two different forms. In the case of in-home caregivers or family childcare homes, the family is the employer who hires the childcare provider as a direct employee. In center-based care, the family purchases childcare services from the center and receives direct care from the childcare provider, who is an employee of the center. The latter form allows for business matters and caring relationships to be more organizationally separated, yet neither type of commodified care eliminates the contradiction of turning caring relationships into paid work.

Tensions between the principles of paid work and the principles of care were evident in a study of eighty-six family childcare providers conducted by Margaret Nelson (1990) in Vermont. She found that family childcare providers were constantly struggling to strike a balance between the personal and market aspect of their relationships with the parents for whom they worked and the children for whom they cared. Family childcare providers often had to remind parents of closing times and overdue payments in order to keep the business aspects of the relationships clear. Because they also cared about the families they worked for and with, they sometimes continued to care for children even when the parents failed to pay childcare bills or honor contracts. With the children, providers constantly had to remind themselves about the risk of attachment and the need to maintain a "detached attachment"—an attachment that constitutes a real emotional connection yet recognizes that the child is not their own. According to Nelson, these dynamics occur because family childcare work is an ambiguous mix that not only involves uncontracted caregiving activities and amorphous caring feelings but also requires maintaining a contractual, market-based relationship with the child's family.

Another ambiguity is how to pay fairly for care work. Caring, in itself, is an unpriceable activity, yet remuneration is required when mothers delegate the care to paid workers. It is widely recognized that the wages of childcare providers are low and do not fully compensate for their time and skill, let alone the importance of their labor. One of the reasons that the full value of care work is not paid is because in many instances the childcare provider's motivation to do the work is viewed as a compensatory supplement to monetary compensation. Mary Tuominen's study of family childcare providers (1998) revealed that some family childcare providers go into this type of work both because they want to be stay-at-home mothers with their own children and because they need extra income. Other providers go into the work because they are ethically and politically motivated to do the work in order to help poor women get ahead. Family childcare providers often provide care at rates paid by the state, which are well below the going market rate, because they want to help low-income families. And the emotional attachments that providers develop for the children is viewed as another form of compensation.

Tuominen has observed that when family childcare providers modify their own contracts to be supportive of parents, they send contradictory messages that contractual and market-based rules do not need to be adhered to and money is not the reason they are doing this work. Childcare providers sometimes feel that emotional attachments and caring result in parents taking advantage of and exploiting their labor beyond the contracted arrangements. They find working with parents the most difficult part of the job, because their interactions with parents sometimes involve struggles over adherence to the contract and how much money is owed in the context of caring relationships. Providers do not attach a price tag to the care they give, and they give it genuinely, but they do not want to be exploited by parents who assume they can "bank" on feelings of care for childcare services.

Given the personal content of the work and the daily contact between mothers and childcare providers, this relationship tends to move from a formal one to a more personal one. In a study of middle-class parents who hired in-home caregivers, Julia Wrigley (1995) found that parents regulate how personal these relationships may become. Few remain strictly employer-employee relationships. The ambiguity was greatest for first-time parents whose inexperience led them to go beyond a clearly defined employer role. Not only did parents receive childcare services from their providers (the formal reason for the relationship), but they also responded to the providers' personal needs by giving support (informal practices within the relationship). Some parents served as financial and emotional safety nets for their less well off childcare providers. They lent childcare providers money, took them to their own doctors, helped them navigate legal issues, and facilitated their access to social services. As Wrigley found, the informal side of the formally contracted service of in-home child care is often personal interdependence between the childcare provider and the family.

Wrigley also points out that as parents became more experienced and aware of the types of employer-employee relationships that could be established, they used social differences to both minimize and maximize the social distance between themselves and their childcare providers and to define or mask the market character of the relationship. For example, a White middle-class family would hire a working-class African American childcare provider in order to establish a hierarchical, employer-employee relationship; they would hire a White college student if they wanted to minimize social distance and operate with a more consensual, family-like relationship. Some mothers are more comfortable with a casual relationship with their childcare providers, whereas others prefer to maintain the formality of the employer-employee relationship.

Even though parents may maintain businesslike relationships, they are wary of the childcare provider becoming too businesslike. One of the concerns that parents have is that the market principles will override the care component of the work. The combination of market and care principles makes the childcare provider's motivation for doing the care work subject to suspicion. Parents wonder whether the childcare provider really cares enough about the child or is just doing her job. Parents also do not want the childcare center or family childcare home to be run strictly according to business principles. For example, when childcare centers or family childcare providers are having difficulty maintaining full enrollment or adequate profit from the work, decisions to resolve financial difficulties may take priority over considering the quality of care. A childcare center director may feel pressure to make admission decisions based on the need to keep enrollment up rather than because a child fits well with the center. During the 1990s, both centers and family childcare homes often had licensed capacities that exceeded their actual enrollments. Preschools were operating at 92 percent capacity, and family day cares were half full (Fuller and Liang 1996). The concern that underenrollment, rather than fit, may drive enrollment decisions is real. Family childcare workers also may not honestly communicate with parents about their children because of their concerns about enrollment needs. These issues undermine a parent's sense of trust in the integrity of care and childcare providers' motivation, leaving them to wonder what happens between the provider and the child when they are not around.

Another factor that fuels parents' doubts is the instability of the childcare workforce. Notwithstanding the variety in the organization of the work—that is, the great diversity of types of child care as well as within each type of care—the workforce is startlingly uniform: almost all female, predominantly low paid, uncredentialed, and with high turnover rates (Macdonald and Sirianni 1996; Tuominen 1994 and 1998). Even in childcare centers, many providers are not formally trained; neither credentials nor formal education are required for nonsupervisory positions. The assumption that caring for children is a "natural" ability (of women), as well as the low pay and low prestige of childcare work, still underlie the recruitment of unskilled women workers. The need for workers, coupled with their high turnover rate, predisposes child care to remain an entry-level position. The low wages ensure that childcare workers will be disproportionately recruited from groups with low income and low levels of education. Because limited employment opportunities restrict the occupational choices of women of color and immigrant women, a disproportionate number of women from racial ethnic and low-income groups enter childcare work. The combination of gendered assumptions, entry-level employment opportunities, racial stratification in the labor force, high turnover rates, and misconceptions about caring work creates and maintains a pool of low-status workers, despite the increasing prevalence of early childhood education models that allow some childcare providers to view themselves more as teachers than as babysitters.

The employed mothers who use childcare centers and family childcare homes cannot assume that their children are necessarily in good hands, since so high a proportion of the workforce is not trained. Although professionalization of childcare workers would allay some parental concerns, efforts to professionalize this occupation are undermined by the high turnover rate of the occupation. This means that many childcare workers continue to be untrained, and their knowledge of children is for the most part based on long-term experiential contact with them rather than formal knowledge of principles of child development. Typically, doing child care for neighbors, working with children in preschool programs, and studying child development in high school and community college classes have led many White working-class American women to enter this occupation unintentionally, and they remain there for reasons unrelated to their education. Young women capitalize on their teenage experiences of caring for young children to become workers in childcare centers. Young mothers seeking ways to combine employment with motherhood often establish family childcare homes, even though they had never previously considered child care as an occupation.

Paying more for the work would give it greater professional status and allow employers to raise the training requirements. However, the resistance to increasing compensation for childcare services is not only a matter of societal disrespect for the work, it is also perpetuated by the structural character of the work. Childcare workers are needed for hours that extend beyond the typical eight-hour work day. Starting their days earlier and working later than most workers not only means they have long work days, but it also means that to keep the total cost acceptable for most parents, childcare workers' remuneration must remain below what others are paid for their time. Their fees cannot exceed or even approach the wages of the people for whom they provide services. They have to keep the cost of child care low enough to ensure they have clients.

Policymakers fear that requiring potential employees to have formal training in developmentally appropriate practices would limit the pool of possible employees, as well as cause an expansion of an underground, even more unregulated, market. The formal sector of regulated and licensed care already competes with the informal economy of childcare services. Licensing and regulations push some forms of care further into hidden corners. Having credentials does not necessarily benefit the workers either; formal training is seldom rewarded with higher pay, given the availability of untrained workers. Only center directors—and by no means all of them—are regarded as professionals. Career ladders in this field are steep and short. And informal care remains strong and persistent because it is cheaper. For example, undocumented immigrant workers, one of the common sources of in-home, low-cost child care, are unregulated and highly exploitable. Entry-level workers are expected to be flexible—that is, to work whenever they are needed—and to be available for longer hours of care. In-home providers can be asked to do housework as well as child care.

All these factors—the lack of familiarity with the childcare providers they hire, the incongruity of paying people to provide care, the ambiguous balance between market and care principles, the uncredentialed and unregulated labor force of childcare workers and their high turnover—contribute to parents' doubts about the quality of care that their children receive and together conspire to put in doubt the major obstacle with which parents must contend.

A New Parenting Responsibility

Because so little has been done to regulate the quality of the environment or the workers who provide child care, parents find themselves in a confusing market of childcare services that often fails to give them confidence in how their children are being cared for. This is not a system of childcare services that is working well for parents. The organization of the childcare system in the United States around private, market-based sources of care assumes a consumer model of locating and using that care. This makes the process of finding and using childcare services even more difficult, and the burden of highly individualized responsibility for choosing quality care and continuing to ensure its quality is an ongoing dilemma for parents.

Making childcare arrangements through market-based childcare services creates a new, expanded parenting responsibility. Parents have always played an important role in monitoring their children's well-being and advocating for them when children move out of the home and into institutional settings (Small and Eastman 1991). Historically, children moved into these settings, such as schools, at an older age. Until recently, the common assumption was that very young children remained isolated in their mothers' care, leaving home only temporarily for short periods of time, if at all, until they entered kindergarten. With the increased use of childcare services for children under the age of six, parents now have the additional responsibility of ensuring the quality of their children's early childcare experiences. Parents cannot assume that the childcare provider who cares for their children shares their ideas about child rearing. Childcare providers are expected to genuinely like young children and provide emotional care for them, not because they are family or friends, but because it is their job. Parents lack experience, guidelines, and models of how to ensure the quality of care in paid childcare arrangements. How to carry out this new responsibility is not clearly defined. Although the acts of care are delegated to others, the primary responsibility for ensuring the care remains with the parent, which usually means with the mother.

The increased use of regular, full-time care outside of the home means that the more parents shift the care of their children to others, the more they need to look out for their children's best interests when they are in the care of others. The ambiguities about how to turn care into paid work, heightened by the lack of governmental regulation and the wide variety of care available, as well as the high staff turnover and the inexperience of parents with young children, requires a new set of parenting skills. The increased use of nonparental childcare services involves learning how to judiciously choose between different options, as well as how to continue to maintain the responsibility for a child's well-being even when the parent is no longer always providing direct care. This "responsibility-without-presence" is still an unarticulated, expanded facet of parenting for families of very young children using nonparental childcare arrangements. Most parenting books still address parenting issues as if parents (usually mothers) are providing stay-at-home, full-time care with their children (Hays 1996). Although there are more and more books about how to choose child care, few acknowledge that the use of childcare services transforms how people parent. Because monitoring childcare arrangements has been such an unacknowledged aspect of parenting, parents of very young children are not prepared when they assume this responsibility.

Making Care Work

Checklists offering ways to evaluate the quality of childcare settings give the impression that if parents select wisely, they will be satisfied with their childcare arrangements. This suggests that quality is an internal matter related to what goes on in a particular childcare setting and how children are affected by that care. However, the concerns that parents expressed to me about their childcare arrangements were broader and not limited to one type of care. Across all types of care, parents shared some common concerns about how to learn what was reasonable to expect in their childcare arrangements, how to evaluate when something that concerned them actually mattered, and how to address their concerns with their childcare providers. These concerns emerged even in long-term childcare arrangements and were experienced even by confident parents. They were created by the volatility inherent in the childcare system—the variety of arrangements, the instability of the workforce, differing values about how to raise children, and the changing needs of growing children. Mothers and childcare providers expend tremendous energy working to hold together a system of care that does not fully support employed mothers' childcare needs or value the childcare provider fully.

In this book, I show how mothers still have the executive responsibility for monitoring the quality of child care even though others do much of the care work in their absence. I present how worrying is inevitable in this context of privatized nonparental care, even after childcare arrangements are established (chapter 2). I move from the daily worries and efforts of mothers and ways mothers manage their childcare arrangements to the political-economic level, to examine how this particular market-based childcare system emerged in the United States, showing the shift away from familiar forms of kin and kith care and the normalization of maternal employment and nonmaternal care (chapter 3). I identify the different kinds of interpersonal relationships that emerge as individual mothers try to make sense of the mix of market and care principles that underlie nonparental child care and develop their interpersonal relationships with childcare providers as a strategy for coping with this political economic context (chapter 4). I identify how parenting responsibilities have expanded and mothers' consciousness becomes politicized when using paid childcare arrangements and show that mothers advocate for their children and support their childcare providers to ensure the quality of their children's care (chapter 5). The conclusion of this book makes research and practice recommendations for how to ensure the quality of care so that mothers can worry less about them, suggesting how institutional practices could be changed to help mothers worry less and better address their childcare concerns. In mothers' privatized efforts, we find the seeds of the ideas for more communal and social solutions.

Even though parents can readily purchase childcare services through a marketplace, their experiences in navigating the childcare system and their responsibility for ensuring the quality of care are still private. Parents have the dual problem of defining what quality care is and ensuring that it is being provided, and doing this within a changing political economy of childcare. The care of young children is deeply embedded in adult relationships and social, economic, and political structures. While this may seem like a statement of the obvious, it isn't. Discussions about the quality of nonparental child care neglect to pay attention to the organization of the childcare options parents have and the nature and quality of the adult relationships that develop in that context. Because of the changing ways families establish and maintain their nonparental childcare arrangements, it is more important than ever to turn our attention toward these relationships. Such an examination is particularly timely and necessary as more and more families turn to market-based childcare services.

One

The Burden of Responsibility and the Illusion of Choice

Since the 1960s, shifts in the world economy and gender ideologies have contributed to a noticeable rise in the rate of maternal employment, even among middle-class families and mothers with very young children. In the United States, mothers have been pushed into the labor force by a rise in middle-class male underemployment and declining real family wages caused by an expanding global economy that reorganized managerial structures and contracted job opportunities in the manufacturing sector. In addition, increasing employment opportunities for women in service and clerical sectors, new technological jobs, and more positive employer attitudes toward hiring women have pulled mothers into the job market. Maternal employment has also increased in response to changing family structures resulting from rising rates of divorce and nonmarital childbirth.

Changes in family life have accompanied the rise in maternal employment and have further supported this increase in families without a stay-at-home parent. As Hoffman and Youngblade (1999) have stated so succinctly:

> We live in a world where most mothers work. It is the norm. It is important to realize that the present social setting is different from what existed in the recent past. The demands of homemaking have lessened, the number of children in families have decreased, gender-role attitudes have changed. Individuals' expectations for a satisfying life have altered, mari-

> tal stability has declined, there are fewer full-time homemakers in the neighborhoods, and the adult goals for which children are being socialized are not the same. These interactive changes have operated to increase the rate of maternal employment. (279)

Maternal employment is now a fact of life in the United States. In families with children under six, 61 percent of married-couple families and 55.2 percent of families maintained by a single mother have mothers who work for wages outside the home (U.S. Bureau of Labor Statistics 1997, table 4). Even mothers with very young children have high rates of employment: 59.5 percent of mothers with children three to five and 60.7 percent of mothers with children under three (U.S. Department of Labor 2000). An increasing number of mothers return to work quickly after childbirth.

As the numbers of mothers who are entering the workforce or remaining employed even when they have young children has exploded, so has the need for more childcare services. Making nonparental childcare arrangements is a functional prerequisite of going to work each day for almost every employed mother with preschool-aged children. In 1997, 76 percent of children with mothers employed full- or part-time were in some form of nonparental care, and 24 percent of families arranged child care by having parents working different shifts (Capizzano, Adams, and Sonenstein 2000). In only 6 percent of childcare arrangements do children stay with their working mothers, either in a workplace or home-based employment (U.S. Department of Labor 1999). Most American children will experience significant periods of nonparental care before they enter the mandatory school system at age five (Hoffman and Youngblade 1999). Rising adult employment rates mean that more parents need to shift their children's care to others, and the demand for a childcare workforce is expected to grow until the year 2005 in order to match this need (U.S. Department of Labor 1997). Like maternal employment itself, the transfer of the daily care of young children from their employed parents to other caregivers has become common practice in the United States.

While all types of child care and the number of children in child care grew rapidly between 1965 and 1987 (Tuominen 1994), employed mothers of working- and middle-class families who were willing to pay others to care for their children have significantly increased their use of organized childcare services, such as for-profit childcare centers (for example, preschools and day care centers), nonprofit childcare centers (for example, community-, university-, and church-based centers), and nanny and au pair services obtained through agencies. During the 1980s, the number of for-profit childcare centers expanded rapidly (Tuominen 1991). Although no single type of care has yet achieved a dominant position in this rapidly expanding market, center-based care now rivals family childcare homes and care by relatives. In 1993, 30 percent of the primary care arrangements for children under six with employed mothers were made with childcare centers (Casper 1996). Nationally, children younger than three years of age are more likely to be with their parents or relative, whereas preschoolers are more likely to be in center-based care (Capizzano, Adams, and Sonenstein 2000).

The movement away from in-home care was initially slower for middle-class and upper-class families who could afford to continue to hire in-home caregivers rather than sending their children to childcare centers (Werner 1984). For working-class and lower-middle-class families, the movement away from neighborhood family childcare homes or relatives has followed two paths. On the one hand, the lower cost of child care through networks of friends and relatives has kept care in private homes (Zinsser 1991). But at the same time, the availability of center-based care (for example, Head Start programs) tied to antipoverty child welfare policy has contributed to increased use of out-of-home center-based care by low-income working families.

The Childcare Process

The selection, maintenance, and termination of childcare arrangements is a process that starts before a child actually enters a nonparental childcare arrangement. The process has both cognitive and behavioral components, including the "cognitive state of awareness—a sense of being 'in charge' of child(ren)—even though one may not actually be engaged in any activity with them" (Leslie, Anderson, and Branson 1991, 203) and the actions that result in entering and maintaining an arrangement. Employed parents repeatedly cycle through several steps from the time they first decide to use nonparental care until the day they no longer need substitute care for their youngest child. First, selecting a childcare arrangement involves locating options, investigating each possibility, and selecting one (Leslie, Anderson, and Branson 1991). Once a particular arrangement is established, daily functional activities include getting a child to and from care and organizing all the items (such as lunch, clothing, diapers, special blankets, and toys) that need to go to and from the childcare setting each day.

Child care also includes parental responsibility for managing, overseeing, and thinking about the childcare arrangement and the providers. Parents also notice and follow up on concerns about the quality of care, make themselves reachable in case the child must leave care unexpectedly during the day, and make alternate arrangements when the child cannot go to care, for example, when a child is sick or the childcare setting is closed. The entire process requires oversight by a responsible party who engages in an interpersonal relationship and communicates with childcare providers as well as other adult family members. This responsible adult has to consider and make decisions about whether to remain in or terminate the childcare arrangement, which in turn may result in initiating a search for a new childcare arrangement.

The complexity of market-based childcare services means that the first arrangement a mother establishes is often less than ideal or that a longstanding arrangement is not necessarily going to continue to be right. It is not uncommon for mothers to change their childcare arrangements, to have several different arrangements simultaneously, and many different childcare providers before they finally send their children off to kindergarten. Some of these changes are structurally imposed: some programs only provide care for certain ages; the family's ability to pay for care changes; or childcare arrangements disappear. Other changes are precipitated by mothers becoming dissatisfied with the quality of care their child is receiving or realizing that their values conflict with those of the childcare provider.

The Heightened Privatization of Responsibility

Although there has always been some support for providing child care for families requiring public assistance, neither government nor the private childcare market has adequately addressed the childcare needs of working families. Although there are established standards of quality, they are only voluntarily followed in some places without formal regulation.

Because of lax governmental regulations, families who buy care are left on their own to make these evaluations and to choose between different types of care. Instead of having a comprehensive public system that fully regulates child care, as other industrialized nations do, the U.S. childcare system is a privatized, market-based, consumer model of commodified care. The current market-based system heightens, rather than reduces, the privatization of individual responsibility to ensure the quality of care, and working families are isolated in their individual strategies and solutions (Hertz and Ferguson 1996).

The privatization of responsibility is even greater than when families turned primarily to relatives and neighbors for care. When still using kith and kin, families could start with a familiarity that provides at least a minimal foundation for trust. Since parents would be selecting from known persons, they would not be selecting those they consider incompetent to provide child care. And even if the chosen caregivers were less competent than the parent hoped, prior knowledge of their shortcomings would provide some safeguards about what aspects of care to avoid trusting the person with. Furthermore, even if a relative lacked real ability to care for a child, the concept that "blood is thicker than water" would allow the parent to assume that some sense of commitment would motivate the relative to ensure the safety and care of the child.

Market-based child care strips this initial type of trust out of the childcare selection process, leaving the parents with only their "on first sight" evaluations to discern the quality of care. Yet, parents are not quite sure how to navigate the childcare market, and their choices are often more experimental than the result of careful evaluation.

Employed mothers need to make sure not only that other people's care is not going to harm or neglect their child but that it will provide quality substitute care for what they would have provided if they were stay-at-home mothers. If they are to fulfill their responsibility as the child's mother successfully, they need to feel comfortable with the quality of the alternative care. Most mothers cannot simply drop off their children, forget about them, and pick them up many hours later. Employed mothers care about the well-being of their children even when they are not with them. They worry whether they can expect high-quality care from hired providers and if it is realistic to believe that they can oversee and manage their child's care from afar.

I learned that the viewpoint that parenting is a privatized responsibility creates the notion that one's childcare arrangement is also a private matter. Parents are told by referral agencies that choosing the right arrangement and ensuring the right fit with their family is their responsibility. Parents are advised to ask questions about the disciplining style and the curricular opportunities, to observe the types of materials and the conditions of the physical and social environment, to check the daily schedule, and to judge the childcare provider's interactions with children. Parents are expected to evaluate most of what matters to quality care through their individual screenings when they select an arrangement. While parents receive some guidance about how to choose care, much less is available to help them monitor and maintain these arrangements.

The privatization of this responsibility combined with the regular use of nonparental care creates a situation in which most parents enter into the childcare system as individuals unguided by their knowledge of others' experiences and lacking clear guidelines about how to navigate this system. They learn how to navigate the system as they use the services. When children spend long hours in the care of others, parents continue to be responsible for the care their children receive.

Exactly what constitutes responsibility is a complicated matter. According to Leslie, Anderson, and Branson (1991), responsibility involves much more than carrying out activities:

> As opposed to participating behaviorally in a task that takes a finite amount of time to complete, responsibility is the integration of feelings, cognitions, and behaviors and may be more accurately represented as an ongoing perceptual state as opposed to a behavior. For example, being responsible for a child's safety in the house may include feeling accountable for or obligated to the child, thinking about possible dangers in the house (e.g. electrical wires, stairs), and taking action (e.g. installing outlet covers, stair gates). . . . Is a parent responsible who feels accountable for a child but does not think about threats to the child in the house? Or is it responsibility to take corrective steps only when someone else points out dangers in the house? Or finally, is being responsible for a child's safety a one-time "childproofing" of the house, or is it an ongoing state of awareness and attentiveness to safety issues? (199)

Although responsibility can be conceptualized, it is more difficult to determine criteria that clearly demonstrate who has primary responsibility, or more responsibility than another.

Most of the mothers I interviewed viewed themselves as the person who was primarily responsible not only for selecting but also for overseeing the childcare arrangement. Using the market-based childcare services also enlarges age-old feelings that mothers have the executive responsibility for their children—they will be the ones held most accountable for their children's well-being. Mothers questioned whether anyone else was as concerned about the quality of the care their children are getting. Mothers knew that government regulations were minimal and that childcare providers were often untrained, short-term employees. They knew that their partners left the responsibility up to them or were not as critical as they were about the quality of child care. Bird (1997) found that "wives' depression is affected not by children, per se, but by the difficulty of arranging child care and by their husband's participation in child care" (820). Even when they had a childcare provider who cared about the quality of care as much as they did, mothers still worried about how well their children were really being cared for. In the absence of a society that ensured that young children receive quality care or helped parents negotiate their childcare arrangements, mothers continued to worry about the quality of their childcare arrangements even if they viewed letting others care for their children as legitimate.

Of the thirty-nine mothers in this study who lived with partners, only one mother said her partner took greater responsibility for the childcare arrangements than she did. Frances Trudeau, who held a more prestigious and inflexible job than her lesbian partner, said her partner worried more about the quality of care so she felt it was better if her partner screened the various childcare arrangements before asking her for input. Only three mothers reported they felt they shared the responsibility equally with their partners. Two—like Frances—were in lesbian couples, and one was self-employed, worked with her husband in their home, and coordinated an elaborate arrangement of in-home care with a group of college-aged women.

The rest of the mothers, all in heterosexual partnerships, felt they bore the primary responsibility for their childcare arrangements. If the wrong childcare arrangement was chosen, it was their fault. When they could not take their children to care, it was their responsibility to find alternative arrangements. If there were problems with their childcare arrangements, they were the first to notice them. If there were concerns about the quality of care, they were the ones who worried first and most about them. This sense of being in charge, and also being the one who kept a constant eye on their childcare arrangements, is what made mothers feel they had the burden of "executive responsibility" for child care. Even though others carried out the actual daily hands-on care of children, mothers maintained the executive responsibility for overseeing the arrangements and monitoring the quality of care.

That this responsibility fell to mothers was evident when regular childcare arrangements could not be used. Mothers were responsible for finding temporary alternative arrangements, even when it was not their jobs that created the need. For example, when Gretchen Hall's husband's schedule changed, she took responsibility for contacting the childcare provider and working out new arrangements: "He had gotten a phone call that his partner's niece had died and [the partner] could not come into work that morning. And [my husband] had to come in in the morning instead of the evening shift. So he had to wake up at five in the morning. So we weren't prepared for this. So I had to call [the family childcare provider] up and ask her if this was okay [to bring the baby in earlier than scheduled]."

Employed mothers retained this responsibility because they were hesitant to relinquish the selection of nonmaternal care to their partners (if they have one). Jana Swift could not conceive how the selection of a childcare arrangement could be shared. She felt that only one person could really investigate the childcare options, and she wanted to be that person. She said, "It's hard to say how you could really do it to together. I don't really know really what else [my husband] could have done, either. If he had done all the leg work and had all the people and stuff, I mean I still would want to be there and meet the people."

Some mothers did not want to share the responsibility of taking their children to and picking them up from their childcare arrangements if sharing meant losing out on knowing what was going on in their children's daily care. Denise Johnson explained that she wants to know the details about what is going on in her child's day: "I want to sit and talk [with the provider] . . . because I don't want to get it second hand. I'd be calling [the childcare provider] up at night or during the day or something. And sometimes I do that, I'll call her up at night. We'll talk for a while on the phone or I'll call her up during the day." And when Gretchen Hall is not the one who picks up her child, she cannot get that information. Instead, her husband would tell her to find out herself the next day if she wanted more details than he had to offer. Knowing details on a daily basis was important to the mothers.

Joyce Lewis felt that she was the best person to monitor her child's care because she is more aware of what needs to be done and pays close attention to the quality of the care. She said, "By and large, I believe in handling it myself. . . . I feel more comfortable handling it myself." She added, "And sometimes it's kind of like, well, if I got to tell you everything to do, it's easier to do it myself," acknowledging that she maintained the executive responsibility, even when she delegated the care activities. Like Joyce, Gretchen Hall felt that she was better at collecting information about how her child's day went and this made her more responsible. She said, "You know, I keep track of all these little things in my mind."

Some of the mothers did not question that the childcare arrangements were their responsibility. Elizabeth Seymour said, "It's my arrangement with the childcare thing." She defined her family's use of paid child care as covering for her employment-related absences. But some mothers resented being the one with the primary responsibility, especially when they were worrying about their arrangements.

Both the mothers who wanted the primary responsibility and those who resented being responsible explained that the duty of overseeing child care was what was expected of mothers. They understood nonparental child care as an extension of the gendered assignment of child rearing to mothers, whether they believed in this gendered division of labor or not. Aurora Garcia said that her executive responsibility for the childcare arrangements was something that "unfortunately, we inherit just by virtue of being a mother." Andrea Sawyer echoed this view when she said, "Women have much more of the responsibility of when the kids are sick they stay home from work. When it's Christmas time and the school's closed, they don't provide day care, you either have to take time off or it's our responsibility to find somebody."

Because of the gendering of child rearing, mothers also felt that their childcare providers viewed them as the person primarily responsible for the childcare arrangement. When Joyce Lewis's childcare provider asked her where her child's supplies were, Joyce realized she had never seen the list of what was needed. She and her husband took turns picking up their child, and it had gotten lost in the shuffle. Yet, she said, "I felt bad, felt like it reflected on me. And the teacher said, 'Well, I knew something was wrong because you're always so good about having materials.' And I said, yeah, I didn't know about that. . . . So I was telling them, I said, you know I don't know how long he's not been having these things. . . . I don't want them to think that we're trying to use their supplies."

Many mothers felt that others expected them to be the parent primarily responsible for the nonparental childcare arrangements even when childcare providers regularly saw both parents. Although I heard many mothers describe how fathers were actively participating in their childcare arrangements, for example, transporting children to and from their childcare settings, they still felt that they had executive responsibility for selecting and monitoring the care.

Selecting a Childcare Arrangement

One of the primary responsibilities of the person who has executive responsibility for the childcare arrangements is to choose the right place. Some mothers were able to avoid the impersonality inherent in market-based child care by keeping their children within familiar social networks and places. Mothers who had at a previous time had relatives caring for their children indicated that they did not like institutional settings or group care and did not trust strangers to provide care. For example, Sylvia Rodriquez relied solely on relatives. Her mother, whom she trusted, was her only source of child care for her first child. With her second child, she was more confident as a parent and more comfortable with leaving her children in other people's care. She hired her cousin, who brought her own two small children into Sylvia's home to watch Sylvia's two. She trusted her relatives to care for her children because she assumed that her relatives' love was genuine. Because they were familiar with their relatives, mothers could also be selective among the relatives about who would best care for their children; they chose those relatives they regarded as the best caregivers or most like themselves. Many parents prefer the familiarity of known persons to strangers when they are choosing childcare providers. Shared values and the comparatively low cost of care by relatives, as well as the reciprocal exchange of care and cash between relatives, ensure that this type of care will continue even as market-based services expand.

Care by relatives was not available for all mothers who see it as ideal. Aurora Garcia longed for family-based child care like the network of working-class relatives and neighbors who provided child care for one another when she was a child. She said, "My family experience has been such that all of my aunts have cared for children, and going to the extent that one of my aunts had one little girl from birth to the age of fifteen and if you could imagine that this was literally like her other daughter." Had she lived near relatives, she would have had her aunts care for her child. But Aurora's educational and career pathway had taken her far away from her family of origin. She had to use market-based child care instead of relatives; in fact, she has never known any of her childcare providers prior to entering into an arrangement with them. She would also prefer her child to remain in a Mexican American cultural setting, yet when I interviewed her, her daughter was in a childcare center where most of the staff and children were White. Her current arrangements did not reflect her original ideal of care.

The process of selecting a childcare arrangement is a complex one: parents weigh their functional employment-related need for childcare arrangements against considerations of what constitutes quality care for their children. They also weigh their concerns about being good parents who try to make sure their child is in a good childcare setting. Their choice is often a difficult one because adult-based practical considerations such as hours of availability and convenience of location compete with child-centered needs, such as considerations about the quality of care and the kind of care that fits best with the child's temperament. Cost, which is a structural factor rather than either an adult-based or a child-based need, often plays much too heavy a hand in the choice. Because most families must bear the responsibility for paying for their own child care, their access to different options is tightly tied to their ability to pay for it. Child care is most necessary at a time when families have the least disposable income, because many parents of young children are at the beginning of their own work lives, when wages are lowest. The coincidence of low family incomes and the high cost of child care often prevents parents from basing the choice of childcare arrangement only on what would be best for the child.

The search for care may be undermined by all the different types of care. The task of understanding all the options is complicated because parents may or may not even be aware of the differences between different childcare options: family childcare homes; childcare centers; for-profit, nonprofit, and church-based centers; preschools versus day care; different types of live-in or live-out in-home care, such as housekeepers/caregivers, nannies, tutors, undocumented immigrant women, and au pairs. Variations in the childcare market in different locales, as well as the enormous sector of the market that is hidden, make it hard to discover where and what all the options are.

After the conditions (how much can the parent afford to pay? are the available hours right?) and a set of options (this family child care or that one?) are established, the actual choice of a particular arrangement requires parents to evaluate several factors at once: physical environment, equipment, and materials; daily schedules and curriculum; caregivers' personalities; racial composition of the staff and children; the children who are there; and the way caregivers interact with other people's children, as well as with them as the child's parents.

Parents may not know how to fully evaluate the dimension of experience, including the distinction between inexperience and experience based on other credentials or extensive experiential knowledge. The ability of parents to assess or provide quality care themselves may also be limited, particularly if they are new parents. Even if they feel confident of their judgment, they may be overlooking important factors.

Mothers have reason to worry about their children's welfare while in nonparental care. They hear about research suggesting that children who are placed in institutional care are psychologically damaged and have difficulties developing meaningful social relationships with others. The popular media and parenting books emphasize the importance of maternal presence and the dangers of poor-quality nonparental child care to children's healthy development. Stories about terrible childcare situations circulate among parents, and in their search for care the mothers I interviewed saw poor conditions that confirmed these horrors. They worried about neglectful care, and they worried about placing their children in substandard conditions where children played with broken toys in dreary environments, supervised by unfriendly caregivers. In their own searches, they saw children sharing premises with dogs and fleas, surrounded by garbage overflowing onto the floor, and playing on dirty old carpets. Some children looked as if no one ever took the time to wash their hands and faces or straighten their clothes. They wondered how anyone could leave their children in those terrible situations. And, certainly, they would not allow that to happen to their own children.

Mothers assessed and chose childcare arrangements against this knowledge of worse-case scenarios. Few felt doubtful once they decided on a particular arrangement. At the start of a new childcare arrangement, most mothers spoke glowingly about the merits of their choice and how it was the best arrangement for their particular child. They had a sense of trust that made it possible to actually leave their child in the selected setting. Mothers found even greater confidence in their final choice by measuring it against all the unacceptable arrangements they had rejected. They assured themselves that their children would be well cared for; otherwise, they could not have left their child in these new situations.

The Illusion of Choice

The market-based childcare system gives the illusion of choice—that parents should be able to find what they want in this market of many options. Even though these servic]{ appear to give parents more choice about where and by whom their children are cared for, however, this is not a system of childcare services that is working well. Though they use these services, mothers are not sure they can have confidence in them in the same way that they trusted care that they found through friends and family or when they themselves take care of their children.

Parents also do not feel that they have real alternatives in this childcare market. During the 1997 White House Conference on Childcare, Ellen Galinsky (1997) of the Families and Work Institute stated that 50 to 68 percent of parents reported that they did not have childcare choices other than the ones they were using. A recent union survey noted that finding child care has become more difficult in the last five years and is a bigger problem for women of color (Sweeney 1997). The underenrollment in childcare centers and family childcare homes suggests that employed parents perceive poor quality as a more serious problem than the numerical lack of available childcare slots as limiting their choice.

Childcare services, like many other types of family care that have been commodified, are suffering from the McDonaldization of care. Like buyers of fast food, parents arrive at the counter of childcare services, noting what appears to be a wide variety of choice offered to them (for-profit childcare centers, nonprofit centers, family childcare homes, au pair services, housekeepers who will also do housework, developmentally appropriate child care, multicultural child care, and so forth). This variety is an illusion—the range of choice is not as promising as it appears, because parents often do not know what their preferences are and lack the knowledge of how each type of care differs from another. They also lack the skills to make the best choice or maximize the benefits of the choice they do make. Too much still depends not just on the individual family's ability to find and pay for the care, but also on its ability to judge and monitor the quality of care.

When families have young children for whom they need to make childcare arrangements, they are in a stage of life when their time is limited by all the demands on them. It was common for the mothers I interviewed often to have made no more than an initial phone call, spend at most an hour in observation, and interview the childcare provider only once—usually with children around—before making a final choice. This was not a time of life that was particularly conducive to seeking out new information; it was hard to seek and acquire new information unless it appeared in the parent's daily pathway.

Many of the mothers I interviewed also did not know how to address their concerns even though they were the employer-consumer in the market of childcare services. When I was a teenager working at McDonald's, if a customer came back to the counter with a complaint about his or her order, we fixed it, no questions asked, because the customer was always right. This is probably stretching the McDonald's fast-food metaphor too far, but given their marketization, childcare services too seem as though they should come with some elements of consumer choice and control. Yet only some of the mothers I interviewed were confident consumers or in-charge employers. Most felt frustrated and thwarted by their concerns, bullied by the market. Few seemed to think they could "have it their way" as Burger King promises. Instead, they made their selections, only realizing afterward that their choices might not, in fact, be what they wanted or thought they were getting.

Ensuring the Right Choice

Even though it is not fully possible to know everything that goes on in childcare arrangements, the mothers I interviewed did their best to know as much as possible by choosing the right childcare arrangement. Initially, choosing the right childcare arrangements was an important strategy to ensure the quality of care; it became important later when mothers worried about what they saw. If they could assure themselves that they had chosen the right place and provider, they could remind themselves why they had less to worry about. The act of choosing carefully shored up a mother's sense that she could trust the arrangement from afar, even if she really did not fully know what was going on. Believing she had made a careful choice had the lingering effect of giving a mother the feeling of being in charge of the arrangement.

There were several ways that mothers could assure themselves they had made the "right" choice: by matching the values and practices of the family and the childcare provider; by choosing arrangements that would contribute to the child's social and educational development; and by finding substitute caregivers who were maternal experts.

Matching Family and Nonfamily Care

One strategy for choosing the right care was to minimize the difference between family care and nonfamily care by hiring a childcare provider or choosing a childcare setting whose practices and values reflected the parents' childrearing practices, values, and philosophy. By hiring competent substitutes whose values aligned with their own values, mothers could indirectly ensure the quality of care. The choice of relatives as caregivers rests upon the assumption that family members share similar childrearing practices and values, and kinship ties make childcare providers more caring. Mothers also asked friends, neighbors, co-workers, or relatives for referrals to childcare providers because they assumed that their own social networks would lead them to find childcare providers who shared their values. This practice was especially evident among African American mothers in Memphis, who chose to place their children in centers that had a long history of association with a particular neighborhood or church. This ensured not only that they shared values but also that they knew the providers, the children in care, and their families and remained within the African American community, which also provided them with a sense of racial safety. Similarly, lesbian mothers in Santa Cruz chose particular childcare centers that had reputations for serving children from lesbian families.

Because of the centrality of values, childcare arrangements have historically often been made between people who were likeminded about child rearing or found each other through local and personal referrals. The use of out-of-home, market-based group child care and the geographical mobility of families erode those assumptions, however. Neighbors and co-workers are increasingly less likely to share values and childrearing practices. Thus, mothers have to find new ways to assess whether child care and providers fit their own family values, philosophies, practices, and cultures.

Mothers asked providers about their practices in order to determine whether they shared similar views. Agreement about these basic practices indicated the possibility of establishing child care on a foundation of shared values. When a potential childcare provider rejected any of these practices, she was indicating to the mother that they held different values and the mother's personal preferences would not necessarily be practiced in the childcare setting. For example, Mary Turner, the mother of two preschool-aged children, wanted to make sure that her childrearing practices were acceptable to the provider:

> I wanted someone who first wasn't going to make me feel weird cause I was breast feeding and pumping milk to feed her. . . . I didn't want someone to . . . undermine that. She was eating solids by then and I didn't want someone who was keeping a lot of junk around their house that would probably just hand like an Oreo cookie to her because that's what they had around the house and she knew that if the baby cried then give her an Oreo cookie to keep her quiet. I had Danielle in cloth diapers and I didn't want someone who was gonna complain about that and say I'm sorry but I only will take a child if they have plastic disposables.

Mary knew that her personal preferences for feeding and diapering were not shared by all providers. For example, her choice of cloth instead of paper diapers was a personal preference not based on inherent superiority or difference in function. A mother's personal preferences about what practices are best for her child are based on her beliefs about appropriate childrearing practices and ideas that she has been taught. Using cloth diapers reflected Mary's view about environmental issues and her preference for placing natural materials against her infant's skin. Many childcare providers refused to use cloth diapers because they required more frequent changes, while some preferred cloth diapers because they viewed the frequent changes as opportunities for one-to-one contact with infants. For many mothers, choosing the right childcare provider meant finding a provider whose personal preferences matched the mother's.

Wendy Thompson wanted to align values as well as childrearing practices. She said:

> Home is values, it's basic, self-concept for the child; they get that from home. . . . I expect to be able to find the kind of day care that supports the ideas [we have at home]. . . . If you can be selective and find a place that supports you . . . to have what you already believe enforced, [this] is important.

Wendy felt that the values of the childcare setting should reflect what parents valued at home.

Some of the mothers ensured the quality of care by finding childcare providers who shared their worldviews. Becky Mueller checked to make sure her perspective would be heard by the people who would be caring for her child. She said:

> I also need to know that my suggestions are respected since I know my child. I have my own personal philosophy of bringing children up that maybe they don't share that philosophy, but maybe we need to communicate our different philosophies to each other—whether different or the same; so that we feel they're not clashing . . . on the basis of this phone call and the short interactions I've had with them, I feel really positive after that talk I just had because basically we're on the same level.

Feeling confident that her philosophy would fit with the childcare center gave Becky a sense of trust that this was the right situation for her child.

Frances Trudeau, a lawyer and the mother of two children, viewed her childcare provider as substituting for her in her absence. Frances described what she expects of her childcare provider:

> It would be what I'd do if I were taking care of him. . . . If I'm not going to be in the position for one reason or another to interpret the world for him in that way, to reframe situations in order for him to see that there's a better way of doing things, then I want someone else to do that.

Frances viewed her childcare providers as providing important moral and social training and sought to ensure that her children received the messages she would give them if she were actually caring for them. Mothers believed that shared worldviews and philosophies would indirectly shape the myriad of daily interactions that influenced their children but they otherwise had absolutely no control over.

Gloria Thomas advised clarifying values and practices up front when choosing a childcare arrangement:

> Because you have to make it clear with [childcare providers], right when you meet them, your likes and your dislikes and your don'ts. And find out what theirs is and if theirs don't work out with yours, you need to find someone else. It's just not going to work out.

Since child rearing involves cultural socialization, mothers who wanted their children to be raised with an awareness of their own cultural backgrounds sought out culturally similar caregivers. Several African American and Mexican American mothers deliberately sought childcare environments that would transmit their cultural heritage and practices. In order to ensure this cultural maintenance, several Mexican American mothers hired Spanish-speaking Mexican immigrant or Mexican American caregivers. Aurora Garcia explained her rationale:

> I was hoping that, given that my child would be in the household for a significant number of hours during the day, that there be some [ethnic] similarity, you know, not that I'm traditional, I don't consider myself traditional, but those values I wanted kind of implanted, you know, issues of discipline, you know, being really caring and nurturing, and her being familiar with Spanish. . . . I liked her, because she reminded me of my [aunts] in many ways.

Aurora believed that cultural similarity between herself and the childcare provider would extend to the daily interactions between the childcare provider and her child.

African American mothers also regarded cultural similarity as important. Deidre Lewis, an administrative assistant and mother of two, wanted her children to be with other Black children and to be exposed to African American history and heritage in their childcare setting. She wanted racially similar images around them. It was difficult for African American mothers to find this racial and cultural fit in Santa Cruz, California, where Deidre lived, however. In Memphis, Tennessee, where the population is half African American, African American mothers could choose among a variety of predominantly African American childcare arrangements. Mexican American mothers had less difficulty finding culturally similar childcare arrangements in Santa Cruz, California, which has a large population of Latinos.

The Guamanian American mother, Nancy Lopata, did not expect to find a Guamanian American childcare situation, but like the African American and Mexican American mothers, she worried about how her mixed-race child would be treated by White childcare providers and in predominantly White childcare settings. Nancy looked at several family childcare homes before settling on one with a White provider caring for children from diverse racial and ethnic groups. Most of the providers and the groups of children she saw in her search were White: "I didn't see any other ethnic groups besides my daughter. Everyone else was, well, to me, Caucasian. They were lighter than Black." Although she had not regarded shared racial ethnic group membership as especially important at first, she became aware that it did matter in her perceptions of potential arrangements. She described how she became aware of race and ethnic composition:

> I liked [one family childcare home] because there was ethnicity. . . . Ethnic backgrounds. . . . That's not something I grew up thinking or concentrating on. . . . But I do think that way . . . I mean, only when it has to do with my child, I guess. Because, I guess, it's because she is half Black . . . whoever is watching her will know that she's half Black. So I want to make sure that they don't have problems. I think that's what I noticed about [the caregiver I chose]. A lot of her children were, you know, you could tell that they were half-Black children, there, and they were Hispanic.

The absence of other children of color made Nancy concerned about whether her child's race would lead to differential treatment. Mothers looked at the racial and ethnic composition of the children in care, and of the childcare providers, and this was one factor that either made an arrangement acceptable or not. For mothers of color, race and ethnicity were major considerations in their initial childcare choices. For African American and Mexican American mothers, in particular, sharing the race and/or ethnicity was an important element upon which they built their sense of trust.

Choosing Social and Educational Opportunities

Mothers' doubts about their childcare choices were reduced when they viewed their childcare arrangements as a supplemental source of social and educational enrichment opportunities that served the child's best interests and enhanced child development. As young families increasingly turn to outsiders for their childcare needs, this new criterion of what constitutes quality care has risen to the top of the list. Instead of seeking a person who temporarily substituted for the mother, parents are beginning to reconceive nonmaternal child care as providing something different from, or more than, maternal care. Rosanna Hertz (1997) refers to this as a "quasi-psychology that emphasizes developmentally appropriate educational experiences for preschoolers who are introduced to the rudiments of a structured day, develop positive peer group experiences, and begin to develop a positive relationship to learning" (376). Time in nonparental childcare arrangements offers opportunities for child development that mothers cannot provide. Preschools have also been viewed as an opportunity for children to socialize with other children. These notions of educational and social development are now being extended to infants and toddlers.

Mothers have long been the target of as well as the seekers of professional guidance in child rearing (Hays 1996). As care has moved from kinship and friendship networks to more institutional settings, professional standards of quality are increasingly being used to evaluate childcare arrangements (Zinsser 1991). Early childhood education models emphasize developmentally appropriate practices that contribute to the healthy social and cognitive development of individual children. What professionals mean by "healthy development" are the "opportunities for self-directed activities through play and other exploratory adventures as a means of self-stimulation and . . . enhances intellectual development" (Sigel 1987, 214).

Some mothers understood their childcare choices in terms of the social and educational opportunities they offered the children. For her four-year-old daughter, Darcy Reinhardt, who worked full-time, combined the care of an in-home nanny with five 9 AM–3 PM days a week at a childcare center, which she referred to exclusively as her daughter's "school."

> If you're going to leave your house and go to work, you find a place where your child is happy, don't you? You've got yours at the preschool . . . you got them there so they'll learn.

Darcy perceived the purpose of this setting in the same way that parents of older children view schools. Having the notion that children have different needs at different ages, however, she only gradually eased her child into this five-day-a-week schedule. When her child was an infant, she started with full-time, in-home care with the same nanny who was now responsible for taking her child to the preschool and picking her up every day. At age three, she enrolled her child at the preschool three mornings a week.

Some parents were attracted by the center's promise of accelerated educational opportunities and learning materials and saw the benefits of these resources to their children. Like Darcy, Jackie Terwilliger chose her childcare center because it would give her child "education" and "an academic environment." As she described how she selected her childcare arrangements for the next year, she made distinctions between the different options available to her. Instead of staying with an older in-home caregiver who was "old school with old values," she liked the childcare provider at the center, Norma, because she was a "teacher." In choosing between two childcare center options, she chose the one that was "not a babysitting service" but would provide "activities . . . puzzles, games, . . . read to her, . . . a speech pathologist," and the center's assistant staff would be "better than minimum-wage workers" because they are expected to have knowledge of early childhood development principles. Jackie recognized that different types of care offered different environments to children. When she used an in-home caregiver, she appreciated the motherlike, one-on-one, loving attention her child got, yet she also pointed out as a shortcoming how hard it was to get her in-home provider to do educational activities with her child.

Several mothers chose to establish cross-race relationships with childcare providers from different social groups and cultures because they felt that their children benefited from these experiences. Several expressed a preference for a multicultural setting, especially if it exposed children to a second language. Bonnie Taylor, an African American mother, viewed her child's relationship with a Mexican immigrant provider as important for developing a global consciousness, which she saw as important to her child's development. This was part of what she looked for when she hired an inhome childcare provider. She said:

> I've always wanted my children to be bilingual. They live in a growing society. We have to pick something to start with as a second language and we hope it won't be the last language they will learn. But this is the easiest for us to find support for in the state of California. If we continue to live in California I believe Spanish will be a dominant language even within the public agencies, in a short time. . . . And I want my children to be competitive in the job market. I want them to be comfortable with other cultures. I want them to be respectable, respect, have respect for differences. I don't think that any of those things are possible without having some insider skills—with respect to other people.

Bonnie used her cross-race, cross-cultural childcare arrangement to provide her children with multicultural education and awareness.

The professionalization of childcare providers goes hand in hand with the commercializaton of childcare services. A new profession, early childhood education, transforms how child care is provided, and by whom it is provided. The development of compensatory education and enrichment programs for preschoolers has contributed to curricular developments and early childhood educator training programs. Recognizing the appeal of educational opportunities to parents, childcare centers are increasingly renaming themselves "learning centers" instead of calling themselves childcare centers or day cares. When parents are seeking care and they enter these childcare centers with new educational materials, and they hear about the educational activities that are built into the day, they feel more confident about the people who are going to be taking care of their children.

Although parents articulated their interest in educational opportunities, it was not entirely clear if they were actually expressing their preferences or if they were limited by the lack of language to describe what they really believed constituted quality care. Some childcare providers and parents resisted the professionalization of childcare work if it meant simply dropping the existing educational system for older children down into the arena of early care. Childcare providers and parents had some conception that the kind of care that infants, toddlers, and preschoolers need is more attentive, intimate, and less structured than what school-aged children are given by their teachers.

However, the emphasis on educational development, even if it was just another dimension of the illusion of choice, was also attractive and comforting to parents. Highly structured, educational environments with clearly articulated philosophies of developmentally appropriate care based on educational research appear to ensure the quality of care more than what is offered by homelike, philosophy-less childcare centers or family childcare homes.

When mothers chose childcare arrangements that promoted educational and social opportunities for the child, mothers partially assured themselves that the child benefits from time in care and is not being harmed or mistreated. Using child care that was based on principles of enhancing child development, even if it was not exactly what maternal care would provide, helped mothers feel they were making good choices.

Maternal Orientation and Expertise

Another way that mothers assured themselves about the quality of care was to make sure they chose the right person to care for their child. In contrast to the idea that child care can furnish more than what a stay-at-home mother provides is the idea that a childcare provider can be more nurturing and experienced at child rearing than the child's own mother. Some mothers were aware that they needed to make sure that the childcare provider was someone who could be with children. Marci Washington warned:

> And I think child care is, you have to have a love for children, and you have to want to do that. Not everybody can be a childcare provider, and to give good care, you have to love children, you have to want to be around them, and you have to want to stimulate them. You have to want to do that as a professional, so that's why that's another thing I think that child care is hard to find because everybody can just go, and just say, "Oh, I'm

going to open up a childcare business." Well, everybody's not suited to do that.

Similarly, Mrs. Jonas, a family childcare provider, assured her parents that she would treat their child as if the child were her own. She described what she said to parents seeking care:

> If you come to me and say "I'm thinking about putting my son in here," I'll look straight at you and I'll say "If your child comes here, when your child is here, it is my child." And I don't treat them any different than I treated my own children. If they need time out, they get it. If they need extra love or extra time, I make sure they get it.

It was reassuring for parents looking for maternal care to hear this.

When mothers viewed childcare providers as more experienced or more adept at caregiving, they also believed that their children benefited from being in nonmaternal child care. For example, Kathryn Ercolini placed her daughter with a family childcare provider who was an older mother with two school-aged children of her own and worked as a family childcare provider in order to be home with her children after school. This maternal orientation combined with years of experience heightened Kathryn's perception of her childcare provider as a more competent and experienced mother than herself. Kathryn felt comfortable leaving daily decisions about her daughter's care up to her caregiver.

Several mothers trusted their childcare providers because they viewed them as providing superior maternal care and they sought providers who were maternally oriented. Cassie Lee Smith described how she chose her family childcare provider:

> It was such a nurturing environment. I think [my childcare provider] grew up with kids, and she has 4 sisters, and comes from a large family. . . . You could tell how much Christy loved the kids she was taking care of, so devoted to them, that's what made the difference really. . . . When you walked into the part for the kids, everything's on child level. It's just, I don't know, there's nothing, there's nothing there that you would have to tell a child not to touch. Nothing like that. . . . Christy's a single mother, and she was telling me that the reason she decided to do this [work] was

> so that she could stay home with her son. . . . And, I just think, that's a big commitment, and I just thought that was really neat. . . . You could tell that it wasn't just a job for Christy. . . . I felt like she really knew what she was doing, and I really did not have any qualms about leaving Franny with her.

Some mothers believed that women in particular social groups had been socialized to be more child-oriented and nurturing. When they went looking for caregivers, they sought out women with these characteristics. Some mothers spoke about immigrant Latina childcare providers as "natural nurturers." Bonnie Taylor, an African American mother, felt that Mexican immigrant childcare providers were different in their orientation toward children because of how they were raised. She said:

> I think that like our sex roles, I think that I feel I can be anything that I want to be and it doesn't have to do with gender at all. I think that Malena is more confined by gender. I think her choices of occupations, things that she studies, that they largely have to do with what women have historically studied in her country. I think that her interest in children is fueled by that.

Andrea Sawyer, an Anglo American mother, said she had hired three undocumented Mexican caregivers in succession because she believed that they were socialized in traditional gendered caregiving roles:

> You know, I went with my gut feeling when I talked to them. . . . Sophie lives in a very small home in Mexico and helps support the family and stuff. So she sounded very responsible [when] I talked to her on the phone. So it was just a matter of just how I felt when I talked to people. Because even when I interviewed Nina, she was very sweet and soft-spoken. And I had such good luck with the other two gals from Mexico. She just seemed very sweet and sincere. She wasn't flamboyant, she wasn't a big partier. She was going to school. And just very responsible. You can be a partier and have fun, and still be responsible, but some people don't seem to be able to separate the two . . . the Mexicans I heard were very family oriented. . . . I wanted somebody who was family oriented. They had responsibilities at home. They had rules. You know, they were just good people in general.

They believed that Latinas raised outside the United States are socialized to be mothers and are more child-oriented than American-born or European women. This assumption about women from Mexico and Latin American cultures racialized an entire group of women despite the reality of their widely varying ethnicities and experiences with child rearing and childcare work.

The opposite assumption was made about European young women who came to the United States to work as au pairs or nannies. Andrea said:

> The big thing was to not get anybody from Europe because every time I heard about anybody from Europe, they were here to party and just were not . . . you know, a couple of gals, one was from Sweden, and they just like to go out and party. It's just like you get home and they'd rush out the door and they're partying and at the bars all night, sitting around smoking cigarettes during the day or napping and you know, you just don't . . . it's okay if they nap when the kids are napping, but when you have that feeling that you're not sure what's going on when you're [not] home, you know, you don't want a party to be going on in your house.

The definition of some women as more maternally oriented and experienced helped some mothers feel more confident about their choices, especially if they observed women doing things that seemed maternal-like. For example, Patty Dawson raved about how good she felt about the older woman when she went to interview her about caring for her child. She said:

> I found Miss Marie, and mom and I went and talked with her, Saturday morning, and we really enjoyed her. She was just a very nice older woman, and she had been doing it twenty-seven years. The very reason why she started doing it, was, because, she didn't want to put all her kids in day care. . . . She loves [the kids]. . . . For birthdays and things like that, she gets them special little things, and, for Valentine's Day, she made them the big old chocolate kisses.

When childcare providers told mothers about what they did for the children, they were providing clues about what their style of care would be like. To Patty, these special birthday efforts indicated that her child would get maternal care, even though she was in a paid childcare arrangement with someone who Patty did not initially know. Mothers felt that their child's best interests were ensured by having them cared for by someone who could give their children "mothering" even though they were doing it for pay.

Intuition

Whether they relied on matching family practices and values, finding the best educational opportunities, or the most maternally oriented caregivers, mothers also used intuition to judge the right choice. Sally Trainer described her first impressions of the childcare arrangements she chose:

> I walked into the infant room and there were two women sitting on the floor . . . and there were at least two infants in each of their laps by choice. They were not holding these infants, the infants had crawled there and were crawling around them and being with them. . . . It was just, I walked in and I felt, it gets down, it's just got to be gut level sometimes. I walked in there and the atmosphere and the energy that I walked into said, "I'd like to go crawl into one of those ladies' lap." You know, and it was real obvious initially and as you were there, it got even more pronounced. It was real obvious that these children, these infants, these people, loved each other and they cared about each other. It's an energy. It's a feeling. Then you go beyond that and of course, you ask your questions. And you listen to words and you watch techniques and you do all that. But you got to walk into the situation and it's got to feel right, initially. . . . It's like you're walking into your home. You feel as comfortable walking into the environment as you do walking into your home. It gives you the same feeling as when I open the door to my house and I'm home. I can go in and sit down and be me.

Mothers trusted that if it felt right, it must be right.

Providers Encourage the Right Choice

Recognizing that anxiety is common among mothers, childcare providers encouraged them to take the time to explore the setting before placing their children there. Providers reported that parents often called to find out if the provider had "space," and some parents wanted to enroll their children in their care without seeing the site or meeting the provider first. Providers often insisted that parents had to bring their children for a visit so that they could assess whether the setting was appropriate for the child. They knew that the intangibles cannot be communicated in words over the phone. One family childcare provider warned prospective parents to come meet her, commenting "I tell my parents this—I'm not for everyone and your child may not be for me." The childcare providers knew that parents' functional need for child care often led them into hasty decisions and unsuitable arrangements. Late one Friday afternoon, Phyllis Johnson, an African American family childcare provider in a predominantly White community, received a phone call from a desperate mother who needed child care on Monday. When the mother said that she would bring her child on Monday, Phyllis knew she had to ask, "You know that I am Black? Does your child know I'm Black?" This was an example of how mothers overlooked important considerations in their rush to find care; there are many less obvious differences that are not observed during the selection of care and that cannot be anticipated.

Childcare providers made sure that they wanted to provide care for the child and work with their families. Experienced childcare providers were quick to talk about the importance of the right fit with both the child and the parents. They have learned through trial and error that their jobs are made much harder when there are basic differences between what the family wants for their child and what the childcare providers give, especially in group care. Carol Prentice, a family childcare provider, pointed out the difficulties that such differences could lead to:

> Another thing that will come up [between] parents and day care providers is food. . . . When we have a birthday party and this little boy can't have a chocolate cupcake because there's no sugar at his house, then there's a problem. If he throws a tantrum, he has an absolute fit, what am I supposed to do? "I'm sorry honey; here you can have this." And most parents if I tell them in time, "Okay we'll bring them a bran muffin with carob on top" or something. But it's not the same; they see that it's not the same.

When childcare providers felt caught between the child's situational needs and the parents' preferences, they were uncomfortable. It distressed childcare providers when they were unable to give children what they wanted and other children were receiving, especially if the provider had no objections and saw it as in the child's best interest. Yet because childcare providers respected the parents' preferences and tried to accommodate them, they followed the parents' requests even though it made their work with the children much harder. Carol tries to help parents make the right choice before they even start using her childcare:

> [I say], "This may not be the best day care for you then, there may be another day care that does that. Feel free [to look elsewhere]." I usually tell all my interviews "Please look around. Make sure that you know that this is the place you want to be in." Because I'd rather have them happy here, than "Oh, gosh, I made a big mistake." Look around, please. And every two-week trial period, it's not only for the child, but for the parent too. And it's vice versa. To give the parent two weeks to get to know me, so they like me, so they want me taking care of their kid.

Experienced providers learned that it was important to screen parents and make sure that parents were comfortable with their choice during the selection process rather than trying to make changes once an arrangement was established.

Executive Responsibility

Despite the increasing public visibility of nonparental child care and the market availability of childcare services, ensuring the care of young children remained a private family responsibility, and mothers were the ones with whom this executive responsibility remained. Selecting and monitoring nonparental childcare arrangements were viewed as extensions of the childrearing role that women have traditionally held and women are still held accountable to, despite the normalization of maternal employment and the use of nonparental childcare arrangement rises. Mothers' own sense of having this executive responsibility for overseeing their childcare arrangements contributed to the continued gendering of child rearing, even as it moved out of the home and into childcare settings. The fact that most childcare arrangements, both paid and unpaid, are made with women, further entrenches child care as women's work. Mothers were still responsible for ensuring their children's well-being, including this new executive responsibility of selecting, managing, and monitoring their childcare arrangements, even as they delegate the actual activities of care to others.

Mothers initially established confidence in their arrangements by using different strategies to make sure they choose the right place: they identified childcare arrangements that were beneficial to the child's social and cognitive development or childcare providers who were attentive and caring. They initially gained confidence in their childcare arrangements by establishing a fit between their values and practices and those of the providers, by defining their child's time in nonparental child care as offering their child educational and social enrichment opportunities, and by seeking substitute care that seems to be even more nurturing than they think they can provide. But mothers doubted, given the character of paid childcare work and the ambiguous context that combines money and care, whether a hired person can really love a child as much as a parent would or would ever fully substitute for parental care.

Two

The Inevitability of Worry

Mothers' confidence in their chosen arrangement was short-lived. That worries would arise should be no surprise: given the nature of market-based care, it is not possible to ascertain all the practices before entering into an arrangement; given the emotional dimensions of child rearing, it is not possible to avoid being concerned about them afterward. Thus, the notion that parents simply select their care right—making sure they fit their values with those of the childcare provider's and making sure they hire competent people—is not going to be enough to make care work. Even after several arrangements or several children, the process of maintaining childcare arrangements required constant attention and negotiation, even when the childcare providers were competent and common practices were agreed upon.

Market-based childcare services present a new kind of dilemma for mothers: the mass employment of mothers of young children is recent enough that a clear definition or set of beliefs of what constitutes quality care and how closely the practices of parents and childcare providers need to be synchronized has yet to be established. The responsibility for the quality of care remains with the actual childcare workers and the parents who use their services. For parents, being responsible for the quality of care without actually knowing what goes on creates a tension that is both inevitable and hard to eliminate. Mothers worried about the quality of care that their children were receiving and how that care was affecting the well-being of their children. Mothers who held full-time jobs felt that the long hours their children spent in care made the quality of care crucial to their children's healthy development. They knew that the childcare setting was not just a parking place for their children while they were gone. Yet, even if they found a place that seemed excellent, they found it difficult to maintain their satisfaction with it because they recognized that they could not really know what went on when they were not there. For example, they were not sure how to interpret their children's cries when they left them and picked them up. Were these cries of normal development, part of a brief transition process, or evidence of neglect and abuse? Most fundamentally, mothers worried about whether or not their children were being "loved" enough by the people who were providing long hours of care for them.

Julia Wrigley (1995) has pointed out that it is not possible for parents to control what goes on during the long hours their child is in someone else's care, or even to know entirely what goes on. Placing one's child in care requires parents to relinquish much of their control and authority for daily childrearing practices to another person. In order for a childcare arrangement to feel right, parents must trust the autonomous decisions their childcare providers make. Leaving it up to the childcare provider can intensify worries, however.

Berenice Fisher and Joan Tronto (1990) have pointed out that the components of care include receiving care as well as giving care, and those who are being cared for will respond to the care they are given in unique ways. Extending this notion to young children, it is obvious that what childcare providers do and children's responses to this care will be variable. Because the child is a human being with a will and presents unpredictable needs that require an immediate response (often in the context of several children in care at once), the provider has to be allowed by the parents to make independent decisions in order to provide the best care possible. Childcare providers must have the autonomy to make decisions about how to care for the child, whether parents formally grant them this authority or not.

Most childcare providers cannot anticipate everything and ask parents ahead of time how they want all matters to be handled. Nor can childcare providers always follow parents' stated expectations. What parents expect is often based on one-to-one parenting; their ways of handling situations are often not applicable in the context of group care. Juliet Bromer (1999) notes that "recognizing differences in values and negotiating these differences in an early childhood setting can be a major task. Conflicts and misunderstandings often arise when caregivers and parents hold different beliefs about a child's expected behavior or an adult's appropriate response. Moreover, many teachers and family childcare providers find that they do not have adequate support or time to work on these issues" (72).

When mothers discover differences between what they expected and what actually happens in care, how do they address their concerns? Do the practices in the childcare setting need to mirror the practices at home, or is acceptance of different practices also permissible, given the different contexts of family care and group child care? How much difference can be tolerated before it negatively affects a child's development?

Even the most diligent mothers, who spent several hours observing different options, asking inquisitive questions, and clarifying their expectations, inevitably discovered childcare practices and other features of the situation and qualities that they became uncomfortable with after they had established the arrangement. And even mothers with seemingly high-quality childcare arrangements spoke frequently about their worries; they were concerned about a myriad of little things, which could be as unsettling as having a single, major concern. The mothers described the process of maintaining these arrangements as inherently stressful, a burden that is not relieved even by a satisfactory situation. As one mother said, "I can't wait for my child to start kindergarten. It's going to be a relief."

What Kind of Worries

The smallest incident can create great worry. The mothers' concerns ranged from basic safety issues to general philosophical issues that underlay specific practices. The most immediate concern was whether one's child was basically safe. A common doubt was about the staff-to-child ratio. Mothers would often notice rooms full of children and scan the room for adults, wondering if the legal ratio was being adhered to. Since this number varies depending on the type of care, as well as by the ages of children, it is hard for parents to remember what the legal numbers are. For some mothers, any evidence that a child is not being paid attention to serves as evidence that there are too many children and not enough adults.

It was also not entirely possible to judge how well childcare providers would exercise what parents think of as common sense until their trust was violated. Gloria Thomas said:

> One day I just went there early, just to drop in and nobody answered the door. And I noticed, I felt, I heard some footsteps that were close to me, but nobody still answered the door so I sat out there a while. [The childcare provider] ended up coming home and she had a car full of kids. And I asked her, where were you? And she said that she had left, and she left my youngest child with her thirteen-year-old boy and some other kids, which is not cool at all.

Discovering children unsupervised, riding in cars without car seats or seatbelts, crossing streets alone, or playing with unsafe items were common causes of worries.

The fear that a childcare provider's incompetence would lead to real harm was always present. Accidents are unpredictable, and mothers cannot discern ahead of time how a childcare provider will respond to an emergency. Elaine Ghio, a young single mother, was very happy with her childcare arrangement until her four-year-old daughter fell off a climbing structure at her family childcare home:

> If [the childcare provider] had called me and said don't be alarmed, Alicia fell and I think you should come and get her. But [instead] she [my childcare provider] told me to sit tight and wait and see how she's getting along during the day. And when I went to her, my daughter was lethargic! She couldn't even talk, she was pale as a ghost and . . . what I would have done was either called 911 or taken her directly to emergency and called me from there. She didn't. She told me not to be alarmed and I just found that really appalling that she had used that type of judgment. And it wasn't like she was so concerned that she called me at home after I took her to the doctor. We stayed there. It was about an hour and a half for observation and everything until the doctor told me take her home for a while. And I didn't want to do that. I was scared because she kept throwing up and kept falling asleep and stuff. So then, the doctor decided to put her in the hospital. . . . After that I started looking for another day care.

In this case, the mother's worst fears were realized; the provider had failed to respond appropriately to the accident and to recognize the severity of the child's injury.

Mothers need to feel assured that their childcare provider can care for the child in changing conditions, especially when the care does not take place in the child's home. If childcare providers robotically followed what mothers told them to do, it also made mothers worry because so much of caregiving involves making on-the-spot decisions in response to unpredictable situations. A childcare provider who lacked the confidence and authority to make her own judgments made mothers worry. Elizabeth Seymour described her ambivalence about the care provided by Cynthia, an eighteen-year-old in-home childcare provider she had hired.

> She really liked looking after children but she wasn't very good on the practical side of, you know, changing diapers. . . . She'd be carrying them along and come back and they'd have wet diapers and they haven't been fed, but they'd of had a great time. With Cynthia, you know, if one of them would be crying, I said well just, I'd have to give suggestions to her, just cause she didn't have the experience really.

Social and emotional matters generate the same kind of concerns as physical safety does. Just as mothers could not predict how providers would respond to emergencies, they could not always know in advance how childcare providers would respond socially to their children as they got to know one another. A common worry was that family childcare providers would treat their own children better than the children they were paid to take care of.

Mothers also worried if it appeared that their childcare provider did not like their children or were not treating them as well as other children. Deidre Lewis explained how she worried about whether her daughter's childcare providers really liked her because she was not a cute, lovable baby. In contrast to her son, who was adored by his caregivers because he was cute, her daughter seemed to be neglected.

Mothers also worried when they felt their child did not fit in or was treated differently by the childcare providers for any reason. African American or Mexican American mothers were aware of and explicitly mentioned their concerns about protecting their children from racism when they were choosing their childcare arrangements. However, racism was not always apparent when an arrangement was being selected. When well-meaning White childcare providers lacked experience with caring for children of color and negotiating multicultural interactions, their cross-cultural incompetence created racially uncomfortable situations for mothers of color to worry about. For example, Deidre Lewis also complained that her son was being treated as a "mascot" at his childcare center. The childcare staff's well-intentioned but misdirected efforts to be "color-blind" were, in fact, drawing more attention to her son's race. They frequently touched and commented on his hair. Even though these comments were made as compliments and in a positive manner, their actions set him apart in a negative way by marking his outsider racial status.

Several White mothers would not even consider using predominantly African American childcare settings because they did not want their child to be "different." One White mother in Memphis said, "I don't want him to be the only White child there." Another White mother said, "Just like a Black person doesn't want [their child] to be in an all-White day care, I didn't want to be in an all-Black day care." They did not want their children singled out.

Mothers also worried about any perceived family differences that would lead to adverse treatment. Leslie Trumball noticed that teachers treated children differently depending on who their parents were. She observed:

> Because of where the facility was, and who it primarily catered to, those with a lot of money, and [those with] a lot of influence were given in my opinion, preferential treatment. Like, "Oh, I can't get [to that child] right now, . . . whereas, if it were another parent [with money they wouldn't do that.]."

Noticing differential treatment and interpreting it as harmful to the child resulted in doubts about the quality of care.

Discovering Differences in Values and Practices

Mothers often made discoveries about practices they did not like through chance observations they made when they were dropping off and picking up their children. Certain practices were worrisome when they were interpreted as inferior forms of care. Gloria Thomas worried because "[my older child] had mentioned that my younger child didn't want to take a nap and she was crying in the other room and the childcare provider just let her cry." That this was happening bothered Gloria.

Questionable practices included those that simply differed from how a mother would like to see her child cared for. For example, Marci Washington observed her two-year-old son standing with his nose in the corner at home one day. She was disturbed when his four-year-old sister explained that her brother was pretending to do what their family childcare provider made them do when they did something wrong. Marci was surprised, because she had assumed that she and her childcare provider held similar views about how to discipline children.

In cross-class situations, mothers also worried about the exposure of their children to unapproved values and behaviors that they had overlooked when choosing care. One middle-class African American mother whose daughter was in a mixed-class, African American childcare center, said:

> Circumstances present themselves where my daughter is exposed to the cussing. And I know kids do that all over, but, I don't know how to put this without making it smell really bad, because it's not bad, because everybody is not educated, everybody didn't live in the suburbs, everybody, you know, [some] people live in the ghetto, people deal with ghetto things. . . . [My child] said a cuss word, and she said the "B" word. And I know she didn't hear it at home. She got it from [child care], and it is the exposure that the other kids have been to, that Kelly is not exposed to at home, because of whatever reason, living conditions, who they live with, what they exposed to when they are home. My daughter doesn't watch dirty movies, she watches *Lion King*, *Wizard of Oz*, I mean, she watches things children are supposed to watch. See, some of these kids down there probably have been exposed to a lot of things they should not have, I personally feel. And, so when you are around children like that, of course, your child is going to pick up some of those bad habits. . . . When you have kids that come in from all over the city, and [from] the different low-income [areas].

Joyce Lewis, another middle-class African American mother, had similar concerns about the influences of the mixed-class, mixed-race childcare center her daughter was in:

> Sometimes she comes home with some stuff. Or like one day I was over watching and [the staff] kept trying to get this little boy to play something different because apparently, this little boy has an older brother, like a teenage brother, who was in constant difficulty with the law and the police coming to his house are a constant thing. And so the game that he likes to play is to pretend that he's handcuffed and tell all his friends to arrest him. . . . Some of it is really sort of amusing to kids. . . . A lot of these kids have older brothers, and so it's probably the way that they hear their older brothers talk to their friends. So in some ways, it reflects sort of a sense of camaraderie, but it has sort of an abhorrent tone to it. And, sort of like calling each other names, and some times she forgets, you know, she tries it out on adults.

Mary Turner, an Anglo American mother in California, was dissatisfied with what she viewed as class differences between her values and the childcare provider's lifestyle, who was also Anglo American. She said:

> [The childcare provider] had toys and things, but the boys definitely were always [playing with] action figures, real violent kinds of stuff, games. Not that they were hurting each other, she always stopped that. But she didn't get it that that would be weird imagery. And I started to notice that the TV was on all the time. . . . My attitude was this was a lower-class situation.

Differences in child rearing, whether cultural values and practices or individual preferences, were not controllable, no matter how carefully a mother chose the care. This created a list of endless concerns. Since childcare arrangements are settings that function to socialize children, values are highly salient even when everyone pretends that what is going on is only a matter of caretaking during parental absence or of promoting children's cognitive development. Because of this socializing function, values are an important consideration, and child care cannot be understood as a one-size-fits-all service.

According to my study, the discovery of differences was not confined to the first few months of a childcare arrangement. Mothers became concerned about whether their children were getting what they needed as their children got older. Parents often decided their children needed more educational enrichment activities, such as being read to or taught ABCs. For example, Mary Turner had originally chosen a family childcare home because the provider's nurturing, warm, maternal style was what Mary wanted for her toddler. But as her child got older, Mary began to worry about her son's exposure to television programming that she considered inappropriate for young children, as well as the constant passive exposure to too much television in general.

Both White and African American middle-class mothers who had hired uneducated caregivers to take care of their infants became dissatisfied with these providers when their toddlers were learning to speak. This issue also arose in childcare centers when less-educated women were hired to care for infants and toddlers. Jane Gilligan, a White middle-class mother, became concerned about how having less-educated, working-class, African American childcare providers was affecting her toddler's speech development:

> They were speaking Black English. It's different. When he was learning to talk . . . he wasn't hearing the same thing at the daycare that he was hearing at home. Which, when they are really young it doesn't matter at all. I mean, it's the contact, it's the hugging, the physical things which are important. But, when they are beginning to vocalize. . . . He seemed to be taking a long time to learn to talk. . . . So, I was wondering, if there was any confusion there with what he was hearing at home and what he was hearing at [child care], and if it was delaying his speech.

As children got older, their parents viewed them as more impressionable and became more concerned about ensuring a fit between their values and cultural style and those of the childcare provider. White families that had hired African American and Latina immigrant in-home childcare providers often moved their three-year-olds into preschools, not just for educational reasons but to also ensure that their children were socialized within their own culture and class. These hidden assumptions are also evident in childcare centers that have infant and toddler care as well as preschool-aged care. African American, Latina, and older women are often hired to staff the infant rooms, but for children in older age groups, the staffing becomes increasingly White, younger, and educated. Not surprisingly, the status of child care jobs increases with older children, just as elementary education has more status than childcare work and high school teachers have more status than elementary school teachers.

As mothers developed a better understanding of the values and caregiving style of their childcare providers, their confidence in their childcare choices was often shaken by unsettling discoveries involving either their own or other people's children. These doubts challenged their carefully built-up belief that they had chosen the best arrangement for their children: Indeed, some mothers quickly began questioning whether the arrangement was even minimally acceptable. When mothers doubted the quality of care because of value and practice differences, they worried. Their concerns spiraled up and they imagined the worst possible scenarios. Aurora Garcia best articulated the fear that seems to be in other mothers' hearts. She said, "You know, I think the nightmare for me was, is she really taking care of my kid? Is my child in danger?" "Danger" meant both physical safety and social aspects of care.

The struggle between doubt about and confidence in one's childcare arrangement is a war between two sets of intuitions. One set of intuitions—those mothers used to choose the arrangement initially—often competes with another set of intuitions—those that warn them that something is not right once the arrangement is established. How easily mothers became unsettled by their concerns is evidence of how fragile the initial trust is and how little real knowledge mothers have of what is going on in their childcare arrangements.

Responding to Worries

While some mothers responded quickly to their concerns and changed their childcare arrangements, I was puzzled by how long it took for other mothers to respond to their own concerns. Even when their concerns seemed serious, they hesitated to address them. Lisa Barnes did not immediately change her childcare arrangements when her children came home with bruises. Initially, she accepted the explanations that the childcare providers gave her:

> They had fallen off of bookshelves, this and that, and the other. Other kids were biting them. . . . "Oh well, she fell off the swing today." And I'm like, you know, she's got a busted lip. . . . At first, you know, at first you want to believe everything that they tell you, because after all they're an adult and they're supposed to be caring adults watching your children, and so you want to take their word for it.

When one doubt became a string of concerns, Lisa tried to find out what was going on. She went to the director of the childcare center and presented her worries. Yet only after other people confirmed her concerns did Lisa take action:

> And my friends, like my girlfriend who babysits for me from time to time, noticed it and she doesn't pick up my kids every day. And when my mother notices and [my husband] notices, then you've gone beyond whatever point that you need to go do [something]. . . . Well, basically what it came down to is I was sort of reaffirming . . . my theory. You know, your kids come home and they've got a bump or a bruise every day in a week, and you go to people and you go, "Does this seem normal to you?" Because to me it didn't. . . . And kids do have accidents, I do understand that, but not every day. And so I go, "do you [think] this is normal?" And basically what you're looking for is someone to tell you that, "no, I don't think is normal," so you can go and do what you really want to do, which is basically tell these people where they can go with it, and take your kids.

Once Lisa decided that her childcare arrangement was endangering her children, she removed them immediately. She acted quickly and did not care that she lost five hundred dollars worth of tuition because she didn't give a week's notice. Yet a long time passed between her initial concern and her decision to address her concerns, as well as between her decision to address her concern and her final decision to terminate the unsafe arrangement.

Many mothers were hesitant to talk to their childcare providers about their concerns. Why did they feel that they needed to wait until something was glaringly and confirmably wrong before they could address the situation? Why was it so hard for mothers to acknowledge and act quickly upon their doubts? What did they fear would happen if they simply questioned their childcare providers? And what are the costs of waiting and allowing troublesome practices to continue when the well-being of a small child is at stake? Is the child at risk? The hesitancy of a parent to act on behalf of a young child in order to avoid conflict seems unconscionable.

There are no easy answers to these questions. One reason mothers were slow to address their concerns was that each mother also struggled with defining the balance between cost, convenience, and quality in trying to find a place where she could leave her child each day in good conscience. Mothers considered a complex set of factors and conditions in their calculus of whether a situation was right. Some mothers decided they could get the same service for less, and they switched arrangements. But mothers did not easily move to switch arrangements unless serious problems arose, such as safety issues or unresolvable philosophical disagreements about care (such as whether or not spanking is used as a form of discipline).

Lack of resources prevented some mothers from dealing with their concerns. Even when mothers realized that there was a poor fit, they often did not have the time or money to change their arrangements. Some mothers were well aware that they were using less-than-ideal arrangements because of financial constraints. For example, Mary Turner worried at her desk about her child and tried to make new arrangements by phone while at work. Not only did she lack the time to take off from work to look for new arrangements, she also lacked the income to change to a more costly arrangement.

But time and cost were not the only obstacles that prevented mothers from responding to their concerns. Mothers would actually pay more than what seemed reasonable for child care when they felt that the situation was generally right. When their providers raised their rates, parents often accepted these financially pressing rate increases because they valued the quality of care and their family's and child's established relationship with the childcare provider. They made the cost of child care a priority in their family budget in order to maintain these arrangements. In these cases, the prevailing attitude was "you get what you pay for," even though research on the quality of childcare settings has found that the amount paid for child care does not guarantee the quality of childcare services delivered (Helburn and Howes 1996).

Mothers felt that many minor differences and concerns do not warrant changing arrangements. For many mothers, continuity of care was itself a value. And their discomfort with some aspects of the childcare situation often had to be weighed against other aspects of the care that they valued. For example, in Gloria Thomas's case, should her concern about racial safety take higher priority than her concern about the type of discipline that was practiced?

The point here is that even when mothers generally were satisfied with their childcare arrangements, they still had many little questions about the care: Should they ask why their child's diaper was always wet when they picked their child up? Where did the small scratch above their child's eye come from? Should they question the way the assistant in a family childcare home talked to the children? Should they point out that the slide was starting to wobble? Should they ask about what the children ate? Mothers hesitated because they were not sure if things were really wrong or serious enough to ask about, even though they were concerned. And it was hard for them to acknowledge that something might be wrong with their childcare arrangement.

On the face of it, deciding whether a concern warranted an inquiry or was minor enough to be overlooked seems like a simple matter, but this was not the case. Most mothers wrangled with themselves, trying to decide whether to bring their worries to their childcare provider's attention. Mothers who hesitated to ask direct questions expended enormous energy figuring out how to make an existing arrangement work. They discussed their concerns and what they should do with other people before they talked directly to their childcare providers. One mother reported that she and her friends role-played for hours the conversation she might have with her childcare provider. Mothers often took a "wait and see" approach, hoping the problem or perceived problem would disappear on its own. One of the most stressful aspects of maintaining childcare arrangements was when mothers sensed the arrangement was not working well and felt uncertain about what to do. Just thinking about their worries did not alleviate their concerns; rather, it intensified them.

Fear of Raising Concerns

Fear and anxiety about raising their concerns is one of the main reasons that mothers failed to act on their worries more quickly. After recognizing that there might be a problem, mothers vacillated between thinking there was a problem and that there was no problem. The only way to resolve their uncertainty and address the problem directly involved asking the childcare provider, but doing so—or even considering doing so—launched new worries.

The social world of child care can be bewildering. New parents just entering the world of market-based child care found this situation especially perplexing. The first childcare arrangement is usually the first time that a new mother delegates the care of her very young child to an adult outside the family network. When a mother first places a young child in care, she is offered little guidance about how to communicate with the provider. Mothers were uncertain about whether or when it was appropriate to express their concerns, how the caregiver would respond to them, and what the consequences would be for their children.

Expectations for communication between parents and providers are highly variable and not well understood. Asking questions may be accepted in one setting but regarded as intrusive in another; equally important, mothers may not know what was regarded as appropriate in their own childcare setting. Uncertainty about how they were supposed to interact with providers compounded mothers' anxiety about whether their children were being cared for appropriately.

Most mothers were thrown into great turmoil because they did not know how to raise their concerns, even about small matters, with their childcare providers. Aurora Garcia said:

> It's like, how do you ask someone "what are you really doing?" Or [say], "I'm not feeling confident with how you're taking care of her." You know, what's reasonable to expect?

Brenda Sharpe did not know how to ask questions about the aspects of care that concerned her. She said:

> I want more information, but I don't know how to tell them I want more, I'm worried about what they're gonna think of me asking. Because nobody else does in the morning. You don't see anybody else, they come and drop their child, and go. And, I'm the one who always hangs around, and I'll watch him on the playground. If they're outside in the morning, I'll stay and watch him ten or fifteen minutes, just to watch him. None of the other parents do that.

From her own observation of other parents, Brenda got the sense that asking questions was inappropriate. When she conversed with other parents at her childcare center, they spoke confidently about how much they loved it and the providers. Although Brenda felt that she did not get enough information about her child's daily care, she also felt that many of her questions about the care were not legitimate. As she conceived of the arrangement, the providers were doing their jobs by caring for her child; attending to her concerns would be above and beyond what they were paid for. But Brenda, a newcomer to the center, worried constantly about the quality of the care her son was getting.

New mothers were also inhibited because some quickly developed an advice-seeking relationship with their childcare providers and viewed them as experts, or at least, more experienced then themselves. The advice-seeking relationship between mother and provider created a type of mentoring relationship that precluded directly questioning the quality of care. Because most new parents are less experienced with children than most childcare providers are, they readily grant their providers authority. They could easily ask for advice, but they were reluctant to ask questions that suggested doubt about the quality of care.

Having experience using paid childcare arrangements and using more personal, familiar types of care did not make raising one's concerns easier. Marci Washington, the mother of two children in a family childcare home, was one of the most confident mothers who described to me her expectations of her childcare arrangement. Yet even she acknowledged that she felt hesitant and uncomfortable raising her concerns with her childcare provider. Marci, who works in a commodified care system as a nurse, said:

> I advocate for my patients all the time, that's what my job is. I advocate for the patient to the physician. I advocate for the patient to the hospital, whatever, financial, emotional matters. . . . That's part of my job everyday. I advocate, That's what I do all the time. Telling people, and advocating for other people, and setting up their care, for what they need. And I can't do it when [it's for my own kids]. . . . I have a hard time doing it with the day care, with my own children.

She even understood that the organization of the services and needs included both financial and emotional matters. Perhaps what made it hard for her was that because she is a nurse, she understood the dynamics of paid care from both the care provider's perspective, as well as from the perspective of the person who manages the care of others. Marci was ambivalent, feeling that it was not totally right for her to question the care she used.

Many of mothers' worries arose because they had only a small slice of information. They were not just concerned about things that obviously put a child at risk, such as broken glass in the backyard. They were also concerned about ambiguous matters, such as whether a single angry comment directed at an obviously disruptive child was justified. Mothers wrestled with whether it was appropriate to ask for changes (especially in group care settings) or to expect more from the childcare provider than what she was already giving. The lack of immediate threat and the sense that the provider's style was unchangeable made it hard for mothers to speak up about their concerns.

Another factor that inhibited questioning was mothers' belief that using child care involved accepting the fact that one cannot ever really know what goes on there. This dynamic made it easy for doubts to arise and kept mothers from being able to determine whether or not there really was a problem. Melissa Berger explained her views:

> Just because I'm paying someone doesn't mean that they're going to be nice to my child, or they're going to give her the best. I mean, you can pay someone a million dollars, but that doesn't mean that when [the parent's] not there, it's going to be different from when you're standing right there, when they know that, "Oh, I'll act this way in front of her because she's paying me." But as soon as you leave, you know, you don't know what's going on.

Because the organization of the work hides most of what actually goes on from them, mothers feared that even if they asked and their concerns were acknowledged, nothing would actually change.

Mothers' hesitant responses also involved careful considerations of how to balance the different needs of all the players—the child, the childcare provider, and the mother—within a context that gave little sense of choice to any of them. Mothers recognized that the competing needs of each of these interested parties would call for a different sort of action. Mothers were slow to act or even express their concerns, not because they were avoiding conflict, but because they were not sure that advocating for their children was in the child's best interest. Mothers feared that if they complained, the childcare providers' displeasure with them would be taken out on their children. Marci Washington worried:

> Is it gonna have any repercussions on the children, when I'm not around? Will she be angry or something, because I said [something]. I just thought

> that for a minute, and then it was fine. But you know, I think, as a mom you think that. Well, if I say something to the day care provider, will they take it out on the children? That goes through my mind.

Even Marci, who was confident about raising her concerns, worried about the implications for her children each time she addressed a concern with her childcare provider:

> It's hard to figure out if I should say something. . . . I worry about the children. . . . I know she's a good person, but I don't know her like . . . maybe she might scream at the children or something . . . or not give them a cookie or something. I mean, just the smallest things like that, that I don't want my children to be penalized because she had a problem with me. Or not give them, or tell them to sit down, or be, you just think of all those things that, because people can do strange things when you approach them about things. So I only am concerned about, I don't want them to take out anything on my kids. I don't want them to, so some things I just let go, because you never know how a person might react when they close the door, and you're getting in your car going to work.

Melissa Berger hesitated because of her fears of what she imagined would happen if she were perceived as an unpleasant parent:

> So, I guess that that's kind of the mindset thinking, oh, I don't want to make her feel uncomfortable because I would hate for her to treat my child any differently. . . . Well, I would hate for her to feel like she has to put an attitude toward me because I've maybe pissed her off about something to where then she . . . takes it out on our child to where she relates, you know, maybe what I've said, and then she looks at my baby and says, "Oh, your mother's a bitch." I just feel like, let me be happy and let me be outgoing and fun and nice, and in a good mood, and then she'll kind of relate that to my child. So, if I'm ever in a bad mood, I would never let them see it.

Norma Ratcliff, an experienced preschool teacher, acknowledged that such fears were common among mothers:

> I think that a lot of parents harbor the fear that if I [speaking as the parent] say something, then, this might impact on my child. And so, I [speaking

> as the childcare provider] have to be really careful about what I say, really careful about how I present what I have to say. . . . It's a very, very common fear. It's very common. . . . It's very real. And, it doesn't matter how comfortable you are with that person, none of that matters. What you understand is human nature, or what you think you have a grip on, as human nature, and it's very common, and it's a very real fear for parents.

Furthermore, Norma acknowledged that some childcare providers did, unfortunately, treat children differently as a result of their negative interactions with parents.

> Absolutely there is some truth. I think there's some truth at all levels. I think that there are people who allow, or who cannot separate an adult interaction [from] the child interaction, and I think the children often bear the brunt of that. That often, they bear the brunt of being the child who requires too much, or the child whose mom sends lots of candy, or the child whose mom sends pants that are hard to button, or the child who . . . I think they all bear the brunt of those things, from adults who are unable to separate child issues and adult issues.

It was not easy for mothers to raise their concerns, not only because they doubted the validity of their concerns and worried about how expressing them would affect their child, but also because doing so would cause temporary discomfort in their relationship with the childcare provider. After she raised a concern, Marci Washington thought her provider seemed put off. She observed, "She was kind of quiet, and I think for the next couple times when I dropped [the kids] off, she was [still] kind of quiet."

Some providers viewed the concerns of mothers as invasive. Norma Ratcliff said:

> Some of them are just very direct, very direct. "What happened yesterday, he came home and say, blah, blah, blah . . . " "We need to process this, can I come back later?"

Providers were also critical of mothers who knew no boundaries in terms of contacting their childcare providers:

> Or they'll call at night, and say, "This is what he said happened, and [I] just need some insight into it, to help him process it better, or to help me process it and feel more comfortable with whatever happened."

Mothers were concerned about how their childcare providers would feel if their caregiving was questioned, which contributed to their reluctance to say anything. For example, Aurora Garcia feared that her questions would insult her provider. She wanted to ask about how her baby's diaper was being changed, but she said, "How do you tell someone that is taking care of your baby, could you wipe her better? I mean some of this was obvious stuff, you know." This was an area that caused Aurora a lot of worry and eventually contributed to her decision to leave the childcare provider for a new one.

Donna Weissman held back from expressing her concerns because she did not want her childcare provider to feel that her caregiving was being scrutinized:

> I guess I had a need to not make her feel uncomfortable with her decisions. If you're trusting somebody with your child, you want them to feel trustable, with them having some autonomy. If you just are so controlling about what they're doing, then I don't know whether they're going to feel good about what they're doing.

Similarly, Melissa Berger often silenced her questions because she did not want her provider to feel uncomfortable with her:

> Like one time, Abigail had a little scratch on her face and I know, she scratches herself all the time with her fingernails. And when I saw it, I almost immediately wanted to say, Oh! what happened to her? You know, how did she get that? But then I controlled myself, thinking, I didn't want Miss Andrea to feel like I thought she did it. So I didn't ask, cause I knew that she scratches herself all the time. . . . I just don't want to make her feel uncomfortable, you know.

Clearly, it was a fine balance between asking for more information and interrogating one's childcare provider about the quality of care.

Mothers who had experience with making childcare arrangements lived with the fear of losing them, even if they were not fully satisfactory. Mothers hesitated to unsettle an existing arrangement because they felt their alternatives were limited. They were afraid that other situations might not be any better and, in fact, they might be worse. As Aurora Garcia explained:

> I feel like I'm reasonably assertive, but in this situation I felt totally powerless. Oh God, I think it was because of the nightmare of finding child care, I mean I felt caught. I didn't feel like I had a lot of options.

Whenever Marci Washington had doubts about her current arrangement, she would talk herself back into it by comparing it with others:

> Sometimes, I think maybe I ought to find somebody [else] and then I think, geez, I could go to a situation that's twenty times worse.... So, sometimes you have to stick with it. You always think the grass is greener, but it probably isn't. It's hard to tell, and you don't want to take your child out of a good situation, and put them in even worse.

Unsure if better care would be found and dreading new searches, mothers temporarily rationalized that mediocre care was good enough.

When mothers felt unsure about their childcare arrangements their usual response was not to withdraw but rather to become more involved. But since direct communication was so difficult, mothers often devised indirect means to learn about what was going on in child care. They would find informal ways to sneak a peek at what was going on when they believed the staff were unaware of their presence. They would drop in unexpectedly to spend time or have lunch with their kids. They would arrive early. They would hang around both at drop-off and pick-up time. They would say hi and introduce themselves to caregivers they did not know. They would make special efforts to get to know the childcare providers better. They would ask caregivers about their lives and make small talk. One of the childcare providers noticed that "parents will speak through their children, some will be very direct, some will use a combination of speaking through their children, and speaking to you directly." But this involvement did not necessarily mean that mothers specifically raised their concerns about their child's care.

What Providers See

Childcare providers expressed annoyance when it seemed that parents did not fully trust them even though parents had chosen them to care for their children. Carol Prentice, a family childcare provider, said:

> Parents generally have concerns like "Is there anybody watching them when they go up and down the slide?" "When you're outside with them do you sit or do you stand when you're watching them?" I mean to me,

> that's concern. But if a person said to me, "I need someone standing by him at all times when he's near the sand set because he'll eat sand," I think they should know what I would do with [their] kids would be what I would want with my kids. . . . For example, if I was going to be outside swimming with the kids—like they were out in the pool laying around and it got breezy, it got cool—you know, I'd take them out, dry their hair, clean their ears out with a towel, bring them in. You know that type of thing as far as this is what's been happening during the day. I'm going to treat them like I treat my own. You see that my kids are well kept, they're not sick all the time, you can understand they get good care. But, you know, you can come any time. I always tell parents, "You want to come on your lunch break, have lunch with us, that's fine."

Providers wanted parents to care about what happened to their children, yet they were aware that parents often expected a type of care that could not be provided in a group setting. Providers distinguished between parents who were treating them like hired help, parents who had legitimate concerns, and parents who constantly mistrusted them. There was a fine line between appreciating parents who shared their concerns with them and resenting parents who asked for too much.

In several childcare studies, childcare providers in a variety of settings spoke of their frustration with "overly involved" parents. The early childhood educators in Carole Joffe's (1977) study were annoyed with parents whom they felt did not respect their authority and expertise as early childhood educators. Cameron Macdonald (1998) found that some in-home childcare providers felt that parents tried to micro-manage their caregiving. For example, they would be told concrete details of the child's daily routine (when and how long a child should nap), and their own time would be managed (they were not allowed to talk on the phone even when a child was napping).

Carol said that if a parent's questions or requests were too particular, she became annoyed with the parent:

> And then there's the one [mother] that will say everything. "When he goes outside make sure he's wearing a hat, he's got his sunscreen on and each shoe." You know, "When he comes inside make sure that he has this and this on." "He only wears this kind of diaper. When he lays down I don't

> want him laying on your sheets, here's my sheets." "When I pick him up, can you make sure his hair is combed?" I mean that type of thing it's . . . picky, you know what I mean? It's like . . . [I say] "No, the kids do not get Spaghetti-O's, they get spaghetti with meatballs in it." "Well what kind of meat is it?" It's like, what does it matter to you what kind of meat it is, you know. That kind of thing really bothers me. . . . These kids are getting a great lunch; [why should] anybody . . . complain about it?

Carol preferred to avoid working with overly demanding parents:

> There are parents who are permissive, and parents who are passive, and parents who are demanding, and parents who are totally ignorant. I'd rather have an ignorant parent than a demanding parent. Because I help the ignorant, [but] the demanding person, nothing I say is going to work, they're going to be offended.

Childcare providers felt that some parents had unrealistic expectations because they did not understand that childcare work was a business. Carol described this problem in the following way:

> It's kind of like a bank. Would you go into a bank and say, "I demand you to open on Saturday at eleven o'clock," you know, it's like I demand this, what I want, in other words. They don't ever say, "I demand," but "I want this. This is what I want."

Even when parents and providers were talking to one another, their communications were prone to misunderstandings. Childcare providers were surprised when they were misunderstood, yet they also understood how sensitive parents were about their children. Norma Ratcliff gave the following example:

> I think you have to be very specific with parents. I know of instances, where I was not specific, and parents were very, very upset with me, and rightfully so. I told a parent, that, I said, "You know, she had a wonderful day today." And she looked at me, and said, "Well, what kind of day has she been having." I said, instead of saying, we really clicked on some letter work we were doing, and we really had a great time doing it, and she just enjoyed it so much, and I enjoyed that lesson, and being with her. Instead of saying that, I said, "She had a great day today, just an outstanding

> day." And mom said, she was very upset and called me that morning, "I'd like some information about what my child is doing, because when you came to the door, you said she had a great day, so that led me to believe that there's been a problem all along." . . . And she was very, very upset, and stayed upset for a while. And it was a couple of weeks down the road . . . [before] she was able to kind of let go of that. But she was very upset.

Norma thought one of the solutions was that the childcare providers needed to help parents communicate better:

> You can figure out the parents who are afraid to approach you, and those are the ones you have to seek out. If [their child] had an accident, and you've changed their clothes, and what they have on is somebody else's clothes, then you can go and say, "Your baby had an accident, you didn't have any clothes, and that's why he was home in those old, ratty clothes, and those were extras, and I know his outfit didn't match," and make them feel okay about saying, "Well, what happened? Did he not get to the bathroom on time? Was he outside?" You can present that information in a way that encourages parents to question what you do. And I reiterate that often with my parents.

Experienced childcare providers understood how difficult it was for some mothers to ask about their concerns. Providers like Norma tried to anticipate what would cause anxiety and explain what she had done in order to help parents understand that she expected them to know what is going on when their child is in her care.

The delicate balance for a childcare provider was to convince mothers to meet her halfway where they could share the care of a child with a reasonable amount of coordination of care between home and the childcare setting without the mother feeling that her role as mother was being coopted. Some experienced childcare providers knew how to communicate with parents to get the information they needed to care for a child, as well as how to make them feel comfortable sharing the care of their child. In order to alleviate her worries, a mother must, ultimately, trust that the provider is acting in her child's best interest. To allow this to happen, the mother needs to trust that the childcare provider knows what she is doing.

Norma Ratcliff adamantly warned mothers that they still have the executive responsibility for ensuring their child's well-being, even if the children are in the care of another person for more hours than they are with their parents.

> Do not just trust, put that blind trust in anybody, not me, not anybody, because you have to always be aware of what your child is doing, and where he is, and why. And you can't blindly trust anyone to do what's right for your child. It means that you're sleeping through a very important phase of his life, and relying on someone else to do what you need to be doing, and then when you wake up a year's gone by, and you may or may not be happy with that progress. Just because you've turned him over to his godmother, or your best friend's mother, or your best friend is teaching him, you still have to be an advocate for your child.

The Structural Organization of Communication

Research on parent-provider communication has shown that childcare providers view parents' questions more favorably than parents realize. Childcare providers dislike it when parents fail to express what they regard as an adequate level of interest in their children's care (see Joffe 1977; Kontos 1984; Kontos, Raikes, and Woods 1983). Childcare providers view noncommunicative parents less favorably than those who regularly interact with them at drop off and pick up times (Kontos and Wells 1986; Kontos and Dunn 1989).

Structural obstacles to communication between mothers and providers sometimes prevent mothers from asking their questions. Even though parents and providers see each other on a daily basis, the amount of time they spend together is very small (Endsley and Minish 1991; Smith and Hubbard 1988; Steinberg and Green 1979; Zigler and Turner 1982). Steinberg and Green found that 56 percent of center users either had no contact or only minimal interaction with staff when they transferred the child's care between provider and parent. Only one-third of their center-based sample had more than periodic conversations with caregivers. This communication was characterized by short interactions, averaging between one and seven and a half minutes per day (Smith and Hubbard 1988; Zigler and Turner 1982). Endsley and Minish found that interactions lasted a median of twelve seconds in the sixteen proprietary childcare centers they studied, and the times of greater accessibility were opposite for parents and staff: parents had more time to talk in the afternoon when they picked up, whereas staff were more available in the mornings. Endsley and Minish also found that 47 percent of the exchanges were purely routine, such as greetings, small talk, or comments about minor matters (e.g., "I finally found his glove").

Even though mothers were at the childcare setting every day, the way in which they delivered and retrieved their children often precluded contact with their children's childcare providers. For security reasons, some childcare centers required parents to ring a doorbell to be let into the center. In some childcare centers, mothers dropped off and picked up their children in a reception area, not in the rooms where the children were actually cared for during the day. Some parents also blocked communication by sending in other people to pick up their children, such as older siblings, or they rushed in too close to closing time to allow for conversation.

When mothers brought their children in early or picked them up late, they would not have contact with their children's regular caregivers because these caregivers had yet to arrive or had already gone home. Childcare centers must be open for longer hours than the shifts that their employees work. The children who arrived early were often supervised in mixed-age groups or by another staff person, such as the morning cook or the receptionist, until their primary childcare provider came in. Brenda Sharpe complained that she could not obtain information about her child because of these different shifts of workers:

> I'll ask them the next day, "Oh, how did he hurt himself?" "Oh, we weren't here, that was the afternoon crew." So . . . that's how I found out there were different people there in the afternoon. I never knew that. So, she said, one of them said, "Well, my daughter comes in, she's a senior [in high school], and comes in at four." So, I didn't know that.

Some children were made ready to be deposited quickly into their cars so that parents would not have to park and get out. Since transitioning children out the door—parking, finding coats and lunchboxes, collecting artwork—makes pickup one of the most complicated and tension-ridden times of the day, drive-through pickup was seen as a service that benefited both the parents and providers, yet this practice also prevented parents and providers from communicating with each other.

Some childcare assistants with whom the children spent most of their time reported that they were explicitly told not to talk to parents. For example, one center worker said:

> We weren't allowed to have any contact with the parents. . . . They would drop off at the door, and that was it. And then, when the child was getting ready to leave, they would call over the intercom, and tell that child to come to the front. They'd be ready to leave. . . . Normally, the director, or even the assistant director would come, if it was a baby or something, they would come and get the baby and take her up front. . . . I thought it was strange. You know, like, you can't talk to the parents and, I am getting wrote [sic] up, because this lady asked me, "Well, how did he do today?" [But] you all not supposed to be talking to the parents. I thought it was strange, and I thought it was real funny. I'm like, well, she asked me a question.

This was not explicit policy in most places, but staff scheduling effectively functioned to prevent communication with mothers.

Noncommunicative childcare providers also made it hard for mothers to establish more personal relationships. When Brenda Sharpe tried to get information, she would only be told, " 'He plays fine, oh, he's fine, he sleeps fine.' . . . I just can't get much out of them about my son." Eventually, mothers in such situations gave up and accepted the lack of communication as inherent in the type of care they were purchasing. Some eventually decided to change arrangements, but new mothers who did not know what to expect accepted the situation as what child care provided.

The organization of childcare centers often interfered with the daily contact between parents and providers. Parents found it easier to talk to a director than directly to the childcare providers when they had concerns; in part because childcare providers appeared always to be busy with children and the director was available to sit down with them and talk one-on-one without interruptions. Yet, parents were also avoiding discussing their concerns with their childcare providers, who were the ones who had the firsthand knowledge of what was going on with their child.

Developing Trust

In order for mothers to be comfortable leaving their children in the care of others, they have to trust their childcare providers not only to care about their children but also to make the right decisions in response to unpredictable matters. Developing this kind of trust does not come easily. Mothers often have to learn to trust childcare providers at the same time that they are already relying on their services. The combination of pressing need, potentially conflicting or incompatible values, and difficulty in establishing trust leads to concerns that are not easily resolved, even by changing arrangements. Furthermore, there is no easy way to measure whether a childcare provider is doing a good job because the long-term consequences of the daily care are not immediately evident since child development is an evolving, slow process.

Managing worries was not simply a matter of finding the right arrangement but also of knowing how to monitor an existing arrangement. Mothers expend much effort and psychic energy worrying about the physical and emotional safety of their children, as well as about the ability of their childcare providers to respond to unpredictable situations. Worry is a rational response to the state of not being able to fully know or control the care a child receives, combined with a sense of responsibility for children even when they are in someone else's care.

The mothers I interviewed varied greatly in how they responded to their worries. For some, the initial doubt about the care was just the first step in a long, stressful process of mental anguish. Before they could ask questions or take actions to improve their child's care, they grappled with how real their worries were and whether they were serious enough to warrant approaching the childcare provider or changing childcare arrangements. Many of their worries seemed too minor or ambiguous to risk alienating their childcare providers. Many mothers were afraid of being perceived as difficult parents who worried excessively or didn't trust their childcare providers. This fear inhibited them from raising their concerns.

The process that mothers went through to decide whether to address an issue was emotionally tumultuous. Confident at first of their choice, their peace of mind was short-lived. Once they get established in an arrangement, mothers were afraid to ask their childcare providers when they had simple concerns about the quality of care. First, the mothers asked themselves if they were really sure that there was a problem. Then they asked themselves if it was reasonable to expect changes. Next, they wondered about how the childcare provider would react to having her caregiving questioned: Would she feel criticized? Would the child be mistreated as a result of the mother's interactions with the provider? Thus, it was not easy for a mother to address her concerns with her childcare provider. The lack of clear guidelines for communication created a "push-me, pull-me" dynamic between parents and providers. They hesitated to ask their childcare providers questions even when they were uncomfortable with practices they saw. They were slow to respond to their doubts because they were not sure whether these concerns were legitimate. And they worried about how to handle their worries because they anticipated that they would be perceived as nuisances and they feared ramifications of their actions on their children.

Childcare providers professed to want to have open communication channels with their parents, and they recognized how difficult it was for parents to come forth with their concerns. Most childcare providers that I interviewed wanted mothers to feel comfortable enough to ask them about their concerns but at the same time resented it when parents seemed too intrusive or doubtful, because it put them under surveillance and undermined their autonomy. Childcare providers objected to questions when parents seemed overly directive, or expected them to treat their child as if she or he were the only child in care. Childcare providers were offended when mothers' requests were unrealistic for group-based care or seemed to reflect the mother's lack of trust in the childcare provider's ability to make the right decisions. On the other hand, mothers who appeared to lack concern about the quality of care also bothered childcare providers, who then worried about how they could best care for a child when the mother was not sharing information with them or working with them to synchronize care.

Mothers need strategies that enable them to address their concerns before worries turn into monsters. In part, this means learning to release control of what they cannot control, but this relinquishment is only possible if there is trust in the childcare provider's competency to care. To develop real trust, mothers need ways to evaluate the care, confidence to inquire when something seems troubling, and effective methods for addressing their concerns, as well as to be able to believe that someone other than themselves is concerned about the quality of care. This someone else is obviously the childcare provider.

Three

From Kin and Kith to Market-Based Care

Being aware of the variety of options, without having real knowledge of how they differ or how to navigate them, makes selecting care a doubt-full process for mothers. Not just one, but many mothers felt this way. How did this knotty state of affairs get formed?

Even in two very different regions of the country and under two different sets of conditions, I found these common feelings of isolated worries in a market context. The two regions had very different political economies of child care. In Santa Cruz County, the childcare market was predominantly organized around family childcare homes and undocumented Latina immigrant workers, supplemented by a smaller sector of nonprofit, community-based childcare centers and very few church-based childcare centers. In 1992, there were a minimal number of for-profit childcare centers in Santa Cruz. A very well developed childcare resource and referral service, "the Childcare Switchboard," and a well-organized family childcare providers' association made it easy for parents to locate family childcare homes as well as individual providers. The Childcare Switchboard had more success with helping White families locate childcare providers than Latino families, though the Switchboard was actively trying to get Spanish-speaking family childcare providers licensed and registered. Several community-based, nonprofit childcare centers had high visibility in Santa Cruz County, but the church-based ones were invisible, known to their congregations but not to the general public. Several of the childcare centers were unionized, and an active coalition of childcare center directors met regularly to confer about local childcare issues. The different associations of childcare workers and advocates were actively addressing quality of care as well as labor condition matters. The local community college trained early childhood educators and politicized a significant portion of the childcare labor force. Further evidence of the radical character of the local political economy of child care was that one center was well known for serving lesbian families.

In Memphis, Tennessee, the childcare market was organized around church-based and for-profit centers. Paid childcare services were highly visible: African American housekeepers were a part of many middle- and upper-class households. Childcare centers were also highly visible, with attractive new centers in shopping areas and other public areas, and signs on church lawns advertising preschools and mothers' day-out programs were posted everywhere. Head Start programs had a long history in this community as a common source of child care for low-income families, both White and African American. Two of the mothers I interviewed were using the same childcare centers that they had been in when they were children. On the other hand, family childcare homes were mostly discoverable via private word-of-mouth and personal networks, even though a statewide childcare referral and resource service in Tennessee was supposed to provide this information by zip code. In 1996, the local community college's Early Childhood Education program had just developed a registry of family childcare providers and a voluntary certification program. Recent federal and state voucher systems were contributing to the creation of childcare centers that were entirely subsidized by federal and state childcare funds. Childcare advocacy was focused on increasing the supply and affordability of childcare services for poor families in response to welfare reform, and the needs of private-pay parents were unaddressed. Despite the high visibility of childcare services, the childcare system in Memphis was atomized—private-pay parents and poor parents with subsidized care vouchers navigated the system as individuals rather than as constituencies of any organized interest group. Childcare workers were not politicized.

Another major difference between the two regions was the perspective on maternal employment. Although both regions promoted maternal employment practices as normal, they did so for different reasons. In the Memphis area, childcare advocates' concerns for improving the childcare system revolved around providing more access to affordable child care for low-income families—a social work perspective to help the economically less fortunate. In contrast, the Santa Cruz region's perspective on maternal employment was shaped by a feminist consciousness, and childcare issues were understood under the rubric of a woman's right to be employed and a structure necessary to ensure gender equality. This was extended beyond the usual ideas of women's equality to the notion that men should be involved in caregiving, both as fathers and as childcare workers. Unlike families in the Memphis region, who collectively cringed at the notion of male childcare workers (for fear of sexual abuse), families in the Santa Cruz region viewed the rare male childcare worker as an asset to the care setting.

In the early days of second wave feminism, family caregiving was presented as the primary force that oppressed women and limited their individual development. It was proposed that in order to liberate women from the oppression of families, alternative ways for children to be cared for were needed (New and David 1985). Nonparental child care was promoted, not because it was beneficial for children's development or economically necessary for the family, but because it was good for the psyche of individual women. This view followed Charlotte Perkins Gilman's 1903 recommendation that socializing child rearing was necessary if women were to become truly equal members of society (Gilman 1903). As a result of these early feminist discussions, nonparental child care was associated with an attack on domestic motherhood.

Because of this association, the women's movement was slow to take up the childcare issue because it was perceived as pitting women's interests against the best interests of children. Karen Skold (1988) has pointed out that as currently constructed the feminist interest in child care is about obtaining public equality for women, whereas the child's interest in child care is an interest in the quality of care. Yet "feminists do not want a social system in which children's needs can only be met at the expense of women's freedom. Child advocates are concerned that the issue of equality between the sexes not take precedence over meeting children's need for high quality care" (Skold 1988, 115).

Organized feminist groups have played only a minor role in advocating for childcare policies (Michel 1999, 278). Another conundrum that prevents feminists from making child care a major agenda item is that transferring caregiving work also pits women against women. For one group of women to be liberated from domestic and caregiving responsibilities would require that one group of women rely on the existence of a lower status group of women to whom they transfer this work. The resulting class division between women is antithetical to the feminist agenda to eradicate inequality, which in this case is defined by the responsibility for caregiving. These competing interests cannot be simultaneously met without a radical transformation of the gender system away from assigning the responsibility for child rearing to women. Given the resistance of men, as a social group, to enter into caregiving, either paid or unpaid, women will be the childcare workers. This issue is especially troublesome to feminists who do not want a public childcare system that reinforces divisions among different groups of women.

Attention to these issues reveals the two greatest unresolved contradictions of women's situation. First, how to continue to be a caring mother when one is making arrangements that transfer care to others? And, second, the thorny issue that the liberation of women from caring seems to require the creation of a new subclass of women workers.

Although many American feminists have recognized the importance of analyzing motherhood in women's lives, they have been less forthcoming about examining women's responsibility for finding alternative care arrangements for children. Caroline New and Miriam David (1985) insightfully point out that mothers are caught between their desire to love and care for children and the societal requirement that they do this work, whether they want to or not. The absence of reliable nonmaternal child care has been acknowledged as one of the main factors contributing to women's temporary removal from the public world of work; this removal has negative consequences for their workplace advancement and sense of self-development. An analysis of how the absence of reliable child care also makes it difficult for women to *not* remain with their young children has not been developed, however. Had the women's movement in the 1970s in the United States more fully challenged the prevailing thinking that one woman nurturing one child was best for the child's development, the contestations over women's employment and the use of nonparental child care would not remain unresolved three decades later.

Care by Others

There is nothing new about mothers transferring the care of children to others (Michel 1999; Werner 1984). Mothers have always left young children in the care of others both for economic reasons and to pursue social activities for themselves. Historically, many American mothers left their younger children in the care of older siblings while they did household and agricultural work necessary for the family (Werner 1984). Upper- and middle-class women enjoyed a more leisureful lifestyle and privileged social status by engaging other women (both hired and slave) to care for their children (Palmer 1989). Poor immigrant women have left their children in day nurseries so they could take classes about American culture and parenting skills (Wrigley 1989; Wrigley 1990). Mothers across different social classes have always sought out and used alternative caregivers because they have paid jobs outside the home.

What is notably different now is that using child care for employment-related reasons has become more visible, and the types of care that are being used have changed. Employed mothers require childcare services that are reliable and match their regular and often long hours of employment. The childcare needs of employed mothers are different from those of mothers who use child care for occasional maternal absences or child-enrichment purposes. Since childcare providers substitute maternal care for significant periods of time, employed mothers often need childcare providers who do more than simply supervise their children. They look for care that provides an approximation of maternal care as well as enrichment opportunities for their children. The quality and nature of the relationship between an individual child and his or her caregiver is an important consideration. Ideally, care is provided by one person who establishes a sincere connection with the child rather than a shifting cast of caregivers.

Changing Sources of Care

In the past, employed mothers primarily obtained child care through noninstitutional arrangements with familiar people such as relatives and neighbors, people who were related to the children through previously existing social networks. For example, an older woman cared for the children of her sons and daughters, or a young mother might have provided care for her neighbor's children while she watched her own. Those who could do so relied on relatives, such as their mothers and sisters, to care for their children (Werner 1984). Many mothers kept child care within the family by working different shifts than their husbands (Presser 1986). Friends were a second-best choice if relatives were not available. Among lower-income and African American families, where rates of maternal employment have historically been higher than among middle-class White families, having other people look out for and care for one's children was and is still a common practice. In some communities, nonrelatives were such important alternative caregivers that they were referred to as "othermothers to the children in their extended family networks, and those in the community overall" (Hill Collins 1994, 55–56). Employed Mexican American mothers reached across the border and hired their relatives from Mexico to come to the United States and provide childcare services for them (Lamphere et al. 1993; Zavella 1987).

Such arrangements were (and are) often made through an underground economy. Characteristically, they were hidden from public view, located in the child's or the caregiver's home. Arrangements were made privately, with little or no governmental regulation and licensing. Parents relied on "personal and community-based, first-hand experiences" (Zinsser 1991, 155) to ensure the right choice. Often, child care was found through a personal referral from someone who was familiar with a particular arrangement or caregiver. Even though these were arrangements made with known persons, this care by friends and family was not necessarily unpaid labor: wages, housing, and groceries were often exchanged for the childcare services that were provided. When actual wages were paid, they were seldom formally reported to the Internal Revenue Service, and taxes and social security were not deducted from the payments.

This informal organization of child care within known social networks has allowed for a sense of trust on the part of employed mothers. By keeping the care in the child's private home or under the eyes of friends and relatives, arrangements retained a personalized, family-like character even when money changed hands. Keeping care in the home created a greater sense of security for mothers even when the arrangement was established with nonrelatives who came from outside mothers' social networks and crossed class and racial lines. For example, cross-class and cross-race arrangements were commonly established between economically more privileged White women and African American domestic workers whom they hired to meet both their housework and childcare needs. The wages of African American domestic workers were so low that even less-than-well-to-do White families were also able to afford to hire African American in-home housekeeper/childcare providers (Palmer 1989). Today, in-home domestic workers are still often also asked to care for children, especially infants and toddlers (Nakano Glenn 1986; Palmer 1989; Rollins 1985; Romero 1992). In spite of the fact that these are wage-based relationships, housekeepers appeared to provide intimate, family-like care in the homes of their employers.

This type of practice persists in regions of the country where women of color and immigrant women make up a significant proportion of the population and discrimination limits their employment options. For example, low-income African American and Mexican American women across the South and Southwest and in northern cities have often been limited to domestic work. Other cross-ethnic arrangements are made between Latinas and White employers in the West and Southwest, and between Caribbean and Puerto Rican childcare providers and White employers in the Northeast and Florida (Colen 1989; Palmer 1989; Wrigley 1995). Working-class women, including White women, have always been a major source of low-paid childcare work for more economically privileged women.

Using familiar, in-home, or one-to-one care are some of the ways that mothers make themselves feel more comfortable about having others care for their children. By keeping care in their homes, mothers know what the environment of care is like. By having friends or relatives provide the care, mothers have a familiarity with what kinds of values and practices will be shared with the child. These types of familiarity disappear when childcare arrangements move into the market.

Commodification of Family Functions

The current movement of childcare arrangements out of the child's home and away from familiar social networks is part of a larger trend wherein functions that have historically been provided by family members are now being provided by other institutions, resulting in a reorganization of family caregiving. This shift in care is one of the main reasons that mothers feel less confident about their childcare arrangements.

Family work done by family members to maintain households and their members is increasingly being replaced by consumption activities that make use of mass-produced household goods and services. Many family functions that were historically carried out by family members are now being fulfilled by the purchase of products or services. Not only can ready-to-use products such as clothing and meals be purchased, but many other aspects of family care are also being commodified, such as housecleaning and health care. Even more intimate forms of family care, such as elder care, nursing care, and mental health care, have been commodified in the form of nursing homes, medical services, and therapy. Elder care and child care are the most recent family functions to find themselves shifting into market-based services.

Before the 1980s, parents were reluctant to allow child care to move outside the home into public spaces, and child rearing has been more resistant to being commodified, that is, transformed from unpaid family work into purchasable market services, than other forms of reproductive labor (Davies 1994). This resistance is closely tied to notions that families are supposed to be self-sufficient and private; child rearing is supposed to be carried out by parents, especially mothers, not shifted to strangers (Thorne with Yalom 1982). It was also understood that public institutions, especially government, are not supposed to take over or interfere with how families care for their children except when children are endangered, when welfare and child protective services come into play.

Demographic and economic forces, coupled with public policy decisions and shifts in motherhood ideology, have promoted the rise of market-based childcare services. First, higher rates of women's employment have reduced the availability of family members to provide fully for a child's care or keep care within familiar social networks. Second, because public policy did not acknowledge the legitimacy of maternal employment and failed to respond to the childcare needs employed mothers have, a haphazard and diverse system of market-based child care emerged, much of it in center-based care settings. Finally, multiple reasons for the use of the whole range of childcare settings have contributed to a growing acceptance of children spending time outside their mother's direct care. These historical changes and shifting ideologies explain why the U.S. childcare system is a market-based one rather than a comprehensive child welfare policy as seen in other countries such as Australia, Sweden, Norway, and Japan.

Reduced Use of Informal Childcare Arrangements

The decreasing availability of family members and neighbors to provide child care was one of the first reasons for child care to shift from relatives and neighbors to strangers. Rising employment rates for women reduced the pool of women available to provide child care. Women without children, as well as mothers of young children, are likely to be employed. In March 1997, 76 percent of women ages twenty-five to forty-four were in the U.S. labor force (U.S. Department of Labor 1999). Even the availability of grandmothers to provide informal care has noticeably declined, often as a result of their own entry or reentry into the workforce (Gerstel and Gallaher 1994; Helburn and Howes 1996; Presser 1989). Also contributing to the unavailability of relatives and familiar friends for child care is the increased geographical mobility of young families. As young people move away from home to advance their education and young families relocate to take advantage of new job opportunities, they usually leave places where kin-based and neighborhood-based social networks are centered and thus reduce their access to family care.

The loss of a ready pool of relatives and friends has forced families to find new types of childcare arrangements. In the absence of an organized system of childcare services, employed mothers have practiced what Sonya Michel (1999) labeled "maternal inventiveness." As their need for child care outpaced the capacity of relatives to fill this need, employed mothers appropriated existing institutions that were not originally designed to provide childcare services for employed mothers and used them to cover their childcare needs (Michel 1999). They used existing part-time preschool and enrichment programs combined with relative care to piece together full-time childcare coverage. The need for employment-related childcare services put pressure on preschools to expand their missions and become full-service childcare centers. Churches and synagogues also recognized the childcare needs of the employed mothers in their congregations and used their religious school facilities for childcare centers on weekdays.

Informal methods of finding care and references through personal networks of co-workers, friends, and acquaintances are still among the most common ways that child care is secured, yet mothers are also now finding childcare providers by looking at newspaper advertisements or the Yellow

Pages, using childcare referral and resource services, and sometimes even through workplace referral systems. The recent development of childcare referral and resource services has facilitated the search for child care by making the variety of care more visible. Childcare referral and resource services provide lists of names of childcare providers, often by type and location, hours of care, and cost. These changes in who is available to provide care and how it is located aid in making arrangements with strangers outside the child's home.

The Political Neglect of Employed Mothers

The rise in the use of market-based childcare services is also an unanticipated response to a social and political failure to recognize the legitimacy of the employment of mothers. Throughout history, images of neglectful or bad mothers have been common, and one of the most prevalent negative images has been that of the "employed mother" (Ladd-Taylor and Umansky 1998). Maternal employment has been viewed as violating one of the central tenets of domestic motherhood: that mothers should be present in order to provide the emotional care and activities that children need, as well as assume primary responsibility for ensuring their children's well-being.

Since the nineteenth century, "good" mothering has been equated with maternal presence (Ladd-Taylor and Umansky 1996). Following the Revolutionary War and into the early nineteenth century (1785–1820), the philosophy of "republican motherhood" (Blackwell 1997, 31) held mothers responsible for the moral development of their sons. The "doctrine of maternal influence" (Lewis 1997, 57) assumed that mothers were the primary agents through whose love the child's moral character would be shaped. This process was accomplished through maternal presence and self-sacrifice where the "mother's mission was to live for her child" (Lewis, 1997, 63). The "sentimentalized Victorian mother" (Ladd-Taylor and Umansky 1998, 7) was supposed to subordinate herself to the needs of her children. Furthermore, this concept of domestic motherhood in the Western tradition also expects mothers to carry out their mothering functions exclusively in the private realm (Nakano Glenn 1994, 15).

At the end of the nineteenth century, maternal responsibility for children was further reinforced by the notion of "scientific motherhood" (Apple 1997,

90) wherein childrearing experts (doctors, social workers, child developmentalists) provided expert advice to mothers on how to raise their children. The "idealization of motherhood" (Daly 1982, 96) which placed the responsibility for the emotional well-being and socialization of children on the mother became even more explicit after World War I in the United States. Between 1940 and 1970, the ideal of a domestic mother was reinforced when the United States experienced unprecedented economic prosperity that temporarily allowed large numbers of families across class to rely on a single wage earner (Coontz 1992).

This ideology of domestic motherhood constructed motherhood and employment as incompatible. Since a mother should not delegate the care of her children to others, maternal employment was regarded as legitimate only if the family were suffering some extreme hardship that made her temporary employment essential (Michel 1999). The employment of single mothers, poor mothers, and other mothers who are working in their children's interests (rather than their own) has been accepted only as a regrettable necessity.

Many childrearing experts have viewed maternal employment as contributing to maternal incompetence, fearing that employed mothers stunt their children's development by neglecting to provide enough attention (McDonnell 1998). Maternal absence from the home has often been blamed for child neglect, dirty homes, uncivilized children and delinquent juveniles, and a lack of "normalcy" in family life (Breckenridge and Abbot 1917; Essig and Morgan 1946; Glueck and Glueck 1951; Ladd-Taylor and Umansky 1999; for a review of research on the effects of maternal employment see Michel 1999, and Hoffman and Youngblade 1999).

Policymakers and the public have not objected to nonmaternal care for children who are believed to be living in families that place them at risk, especially poor families and families headed by single mothers. The voting public has supported policies and programs, such as Head Start, that are designed to rescue children from the harms of poverty. Childcare services have also been attached to programs designed to reduce cyclical and structural unemployment. For example, the 1933 Works Projects Administration's Federal Economic Recovery Act created childcare jobs for unemployed teachers. In 1967, the amended Social Security Act provided funds for child care for present and past welfare recipients and for mothers in training programs. The Family Support Act of 1988 subsidized child care for parents' job training programs. Most recently, childcare services were provided through the 1996 Work and Personal Responsibilities Act to move mothers off welfare into employment-based workfare programs.

Childcare policies have been proposed to provide services for two different populations, poor children living in poor families and for employed parents (Wrigley 1987; Wrigley 1990). However, few governmental policies have mandated childcare services for employed mothers because, historically, meeting the needs of employed mothers, especially those who are not poor, has not been viewed as a legitimate governmental responsibility. Direct childcare services for employed parents are rarely proposed. Instead, childcare subsidies, such as tax credits, have been the primary way that government has supported employed mothers and their families in the past. Tax credits allow policymakers to maintain a hands-off approach that neither encourages nor directs how parents make childcare arrangements. This approach reflects the common assumption that economically self-supporting families have a private responsibility for the care of their own children.

The one noteworthy exception to this approach was the Lanham Act of 1941. The Lanham Act set up childcare centers throughout the country in order to increase the number of women available to fill the labor shortages during World War II. These services were not intended to support mothers who were already employed, however, and they were explicitly designed to be temporary. Soon after the war ended, federal funding for these childcare centers was withdrawn and mothers with young children were encouraged to leave the labor force to make jobs available to returning soldiers (Steinfels 1973).

Policymakers have been slow to recognize the reality and legitimacy of maternal employment. Between 1945 and the 1960s, public policy provided only a "marginal welfare service which did not begin to meet the needs of children or the needs of working mothers" (Steinfels 1973). Government-funded, center-based care for nonpoor employed mothers disappeared for the next forty years in the United States even though the "employed mother" was here to stay.

The government's historical failure to provide childcare services for employed mothers is ironic given that in 1920 the Women's Bureau of the U.S. Department of Labor was established to "formulate standards and policies which shall promote the welfare of wage-earning women, improve their working conditions, increase their efficiency, and advance their opportunities for profitable employment" (U.S. Department of Labor 2000). Even though the Women's Bureau, the President's Commission on the Status of Women set up by John F. Kennedy in 1962, and the Child Welfare League of America publicly acknowledged that maternal employment was normal, attempts to depathologize it were ineffective. Florence Ruderman's 1964 report, written for the Child Welfare League of America, pointed out that some mothers were not employed because they could not find satisfactory childcare arrangements; the report called for public acceptance of and support for maternal employment. These ideas met with strong opposition, however, despite the fact that an increasing proportion of mothers were employed (Michel 1999).

Proposals designed to provide childcare services to meet the needs of employed parents, especially mothers, have not been successful. Any policy providing child care for employed mothers was opposed by those who feared it would move women away from motherhood and marriage. These include the 1969 Family Assistance Plan, which would have provided child care for poor working mothers; the Comprehensive Child Development Act of 1971, which was designed to provide child care for the working poor and the middle class on a sliding fee scale; and the 1971 Childcare Services Act, which would have created a corporation to lend money to local groups providing child care.

In 1970, the first national conference on child care identified the lack of childcare services as one of the major problems facing American families and argued that child care was not a special need of marginal populations but rather an issue involving many families. It was a major surprise and step backward when President Richard Nixon vetoed the Comprehensive Child Development Act of 1971. This bipartisan act had been proposed by Representative John Brademas (Democrat of Illinois) and Senator Walter Mondale (Democrat of Minnesota) and approved by both houses, but President Nixon and congressional critics believed that the act would shift the child rearing responsibility from parents to government, and that the privacy of American families would be undermined by nonparental childcare services. Nixon's veto, which Congress did not override, reflected Americans' deep commitment to the ideology of the private, self-contained family, even as family structures were changing. By the 1970s, dual-earner families with employed mothers had become the most common type of household in the United States. Nonetheless, public resistance to mothers' employment was still strong enough to defeat several childcare bills that would have directly assisted employed families with their childcare needs.

During the 1980s, the dominant childcare policy perspective continued to promote "the privacy of the family and the primacy of parental rights and obligations in raising children" and "getting the government 'off the back of the people' " (Jacobs and Davies 1994, 10). This view was reinforced by concerns that maternal employment would harm the mother-child bond. In the late 1980s, research that received a great deal of publicity reported that children who spent twenty or more hours in care per week during their first year of life were more likely to be insecurely attached to their mother (Belsky and Rovine 1988). This research examined how children responded when they were placed in an unfamiliar room, encountered a stranger, and experienced two brief separations from their mothers (the Ainsworth Strange Situation Task). The mother-child bond was assessed by observing how and if the baby sought comfort from the mother in response to these anxiety-producing situations. A child who had a secure attachment to his/her mother would seek out and be easily comforted by his/her mother. It was hypothesized that this ability to achieve a secure attachment in this primary relationship undergirded all other social relationships that children would form in later life. Researchers did not take into account that children in care may develop greater independence or develop a larger group of attachment figures because they are exposed to alternative caregivers more than children who remain in dyadic mother-child care.

Nevertheless, these ideas prevented public acknowledgment that maternal employment was legitimate, and even retarded general recognition of the widespread nature of maternal employment. The few successful policies provided only minimal and indirect support of the childcare needs of employed parents. The Dependent Care Assistance Plan of 1981 and the Child and Dependent Tax Credit of 1990 encouraged employers to construct childcare facilities in the private sector and helped employed parents with out-of-pocket childcare expenses. These tax credits represented a small step in the direction of viewing nonparental child care as a legitimate, public responsibility. However, the tax credit represented only a small proportion of what parents paid for childcare services, and it was available only to parents who itemized their tax returns, so the program did not help parents with lower incomes. In short, childcare needs were still viewed as the private responsibility of individual families that should be met with little government intervention, except when children were put at risk by families not able enough to maintain themselves.

By 1990, the number of childcare "slots" lagged behind the demand for childcare services as maternal employment steadily expanded. This demand was a social and economic force that shifted children into market-based care. The idea that government should not intervene in the childcare needs of private families began to erode when the demand for childcare services outpaced the supply and discoveries of poor-quality settings attracted the attention of policymakers. Only then were politicians willing to acknowledge that many American children were spending time in childcare arrangements while their parents work.

Even though childcare policy for employed parents has been brought to the table, it was not until January 1995 that the Childcare Bureau was established in the Administration for Children and Families, Department of Health and Human Services, to administer federal childcare programs to states, territories, and tribes for low-income, working families. The Bureau has since initiated a variety of activities to improve the quality, availability, and affordability of childcare services across the country, which for the first time were geared toward all working families, not just poor families.

In 1997, the White House Conference on Childcare formally shifted the debate from whether children should be in care to what kind of care should be provided and by whom. By shifting the public discussion away from whether mothers should be working to how the quality of care could be improved, national attention began to focus on supporting working families through creating quality childcare programs. The argument for quality care is based on the promotion of healthy child development as well as on strengthening the family so parents can provide positive childrearing environments for their children, regardless of whether they work or not. And for those parents who do work, the goal is to support working families who are struggling with the dual pressures of work and family.

This public policy shift is very recent, and employed parents are still making their own childcare arrangements privately. The reality of this new cultural context of maternal employment stands in sharp contrast to the gender ideology of domestic motherhood and the disappearing cultural milieu of stay-at-home mothers that presented maternal employment as contradicting, even violating, what mothers are supposed to do.

Stopgap Responses to the Demand for Childcare Services

During the twenty-five years of neglect that were largely a result of ambivalence about the role of government in providing childcare services for working families, the "paucity of public programs opened up a huge market for commercial centers and private home providers seeking to offer care at a profit" (Michel 1999, 183). While many of these were independent businesses, childcare chains and franchises were also established during this time, many of them built right in the midst of suburban housing (Michel 1999). A new market of for-profit childcare services became an important component of the U.S. political economy of child care.

Corporations responded to the demand created by the absence of a governmental response by offering their middle-class employees on-site childcare centers, childcare subsidies, and help with locating childcare arrangements (Haas 1999). From 1982 to 1990, the number of employers offering childcare services expanded from 600 to 5,600 companies (Galinsky et al. 1994). From the employers' perspective, providing childcare services is a way to ensure a stable, high-quality workforce, enhanced productivity, and retention of valuable employees when they start having families (Rubin 1997). Hospitals, with their large, heavily female labor force, are a notable example. Some corporations that did not provide childcare services began to provide resource and referral services and childcare vouchers to their employees (Michel 1999).

The market-based character of childcare services has intensified as family childcare homes have become more businesslike. Historically, most family childcare homes have been established by mothers who wanted to be at home while their own children were young but needed some source of income or wanted to help other mothers who were employed outside their homes. The complementary relationship between the mother who wanted to be at home and the mother who worked outside the home was based on familiarity and shared social networks.

While many family childcare homes are set up for the same reasons today, the employed mothers who now use them often do not know the providers beforehand. Although family childcare homes are still out of sight in private neighborhoods, referral services help parents locate them. These family childcare homes are increasingly operating like small businesses, and family childcare providers see themselves more as owners and managers of small businesses. Family childcare associations advise family childcare providers on how to set up their homes as small businesses and establish contractual relationships with the families they serve (Stockinger 2000).

Agreements between labor unions and businesses have contributed to the expansion and use of market-based child care. Unions have a long history of negotiating with employers for childcare benefits, beginning in the 1920s in the apparel industry. Benefits have included cash vouchers for childcare, summer camps, and employer-provided resource and referral services. The purpose of these benefits is to help working parents balance work and family; providing affordable and high-quality child care enables parents to be productive workers (Fried 1987). In the 1980s, with support from the Coalition of Labor Union Women (CLUW), unions such as the Amalgamated Clothing and Textile Workers' Union (ACTWU), representing heavily female occupations, bargained for childcare services and benefits for their constituency.

Despite the increased visibility and availability of a market-based childcare system, the childcare industry remains relatively unregulated. Indeed, the proliferation of commercial childcare services that are almost entirely outside public regulations is an unanticipated consequence of governmental inattention to child care. The lack of substantial regulations and effective national guidelines to regulate and license childcare services made it relatively easy to set up a family childcare home or childcare center. Commercial child care proliferated and a highly unregulated, private market-based childcare system emerged. State licensing requirements and regulations ensure only the most basic environmental standards, criminal record checks, and staff-to-child ratios. However, they do not set standards for the content and quality of care. Instead of promoting child development, current regulations attempt only to protect the child from basic harms (Gallagher, Rooney, and Campbell 2000). Advocacy organizations such as the National Association for the Education of Young Children (NAEYC) have attempted to increase standards by establishing guidelines that address the quality of care and offering voluntary accreditation to childcare centers that meet them. Accreditation is becoming increasingly popular, but it is still not common, and many parents do not know enough to ask if a center is NAEYC accredited or what that might mean to the quality of care their child receives.

Policymakers have resisted efforts to regulate nonparental child care, just as they have been reluctant to support it with public funds and policies. Their slow response reflects the continuing belief that child care, whether done by the child's parents or by others, is a family responsibility located in a private domain that government should not take on or interfere with. Since market-based childcare services have proliferated with minimal regulation, there is a great deal of variety from which parents can choose. No longer hidden in private homes, childcare centers are highly visible on main roads, alongside shopping malls and fast food restaurants. The new market of childcare services has transformed the meaning of all these forms of care. Employed parents can now find care much more readily through market-based systems of care than they could just twenty years ago.

The New Acceptability of Nonmaternal Care

Until recently, the ideological unacceptability of nonmaternal care has also rendered the childcare needs of employed mothers invisible, seemingly less worthy of attention by researchers and policymakers. This historical neglect in combination with the more recent acceptability of maternal employment and nonmaternal care for children explains why there is a highly visible yet privatized market of childcare services.

Even though policymakers did not accept maternal employment as legitimate, working families did. Because policymakers did not respond to the need for childcare services, the demand was met by a private market. The increased use of market-based child care could not have happened without a general acceptance of children spending time outside their mother's care. Without this shift in definition of maternal responsibilities and new understandings of children's development, mothers would have continued to hide their employment-related childcare needs in informal networks of care. Because of this change in what is expected of mothers, market-based child care has come to be viewed as a legitimate form of care for young children.

Views about the appropriateness of maternal employment have shifted dramatically in the United States in the last twenty years. The original assumptions that being a mother and an employee are antithetical and that good mothers are always with their children have given way to a greater acceptance of maternal employment and children spending time away from their mothers. The image of the employed mother as a bad mother has faded.

Studies of working-class women's history have shown that poor women, including women of color, have simply not been offered the life circumstances to forego involvement in income-producing activities, either inside or outside their homes (Nakano Glenn 1994). Instead, work and family have historically been interwoven for women of color: mothering has included not only caring for their families at home but also laboring for wages in their own homes, in White women's households, and elsewhere outside the home (Hill Collins 1994). Similarly, working-class White women have defined their wage-earning activities as part of their maternal responsibilities rather than in opposition to motherhood (Rose 1998; Segura 1994). Despite this historical reality of maternal employment, employed mothers were rendered invisible until the 1970s (Garey 1999).

Maternal employment became common among middle-class families during the 1970s. As maternal employment moved into the middle class, working-class women's history became the experience of most women, across all classes and racial ethnic groups. During the 1980s, researchers and journalists paid attention to the problems of middle-class women as they learned how to combine work and family. The American public was introduced to the image of professionally employed mothers, and this contributed to the increasing legitimacy of maternal employment.

Recent changes in welfare policy have also contributed to the notion that maternal employment, even for mothers of very young children, is acceptable. When Aid to Families with Dependent Children (AFDC) was first established, African American and Latina women were often excluded from eligibility for welfare benefits because they were defined as "employable mothers" (Chang 1994; Quadagno 1994). More recently, this view of "employable mothers" has been extended to all poor women, including White mothers. The new welfare policy that transforms welfare into Workfare requires mothers receiving benefits to be employed and to place their children in nonmaternal care. Accompanying this policy change has been a significant increase in the provision of childcare services and subsidies. Rather than reinforcing old notions wherein maternal presence trumps self-sufficiency in shaping policy, this new policy is premised on the understanding that maternal income earning can take priority over maternal presence in child rearing.

Whereas in the 1960s the employed mother was viewed as a new social phenomenon, today, the stay-at-home mother is seen as more remarkable. Mothers who have chosen to leave their jobs complain that they receive little cultural support. Middle-class as well as low-income mothers are in the labor force. Mothers are surrounded by other employed mothers. Young women are increasingly planning to be employed even after the birth of their first child, and their plans are supported by an increasingly visible workforce of employed mothers (Machung 1989). Furthermore, the suggestion that "mommy tracks" be established in the corporate workforce (Schwartz 1989) is a public response to private problems that further promotes the acceptability of maternal employment, even if it also promotes a secondary-tier status for professional women.

Changing perceptions of the acceptability of maternal employment contribute to normalization of maternal employment: employed motherhood now appears customary rather than deviant. Children's time away from their mothers is not viewed as problematic. This acceptance facilitates the use of market-based childcare services, especially center-based care that promises to provide children with enrichment opportunities.

New Perceptions of Center Care

What is also contributing to the rise of market-based childcare services is the new perception of center-based child care as positive for child development. Childcare centers are not new, but in the past, childcare centers have been avoided both by middle-class women, who viewed them as serving poor children and their families, and by poor and racial ethnic women, who viewed the centers as being run by middle-class professionals and social service agencies and biased against poor working mothers and women of color (Michel 1999).

Childcare centers did not originate to serve employed parents; group care was first developed to meet the needs of poor children, regardless of whether or not their parents were employed (Steinfels 1973; Wrigley 1990).

In the mid nineteenth century, day nurseries were set up to serve the children of impoverished families. These charity-supported programs were designed as temporary assistance to families experiencing a crisis, not chronic financial hardship (Michel 1999). Childcare services were often provided alongside employment training and opportunities for the poorest and neediest mothers, such as those who worked out of economic necessity because they were widowed or because their husbands were unable to support their families due to disability or chronic illness (Michel 1999; Steinfels 1973). They were not designed to provide full-time, extended care to cover women's working hours.

The middle-class philosophy of temporary support was at odds with working-class women's views that their wage-earning activities were part of their maternal responsibilities rather than opposed to them (Rose 1998; Segura 1994). An example of this class difference was reflected in the philosophy and practices of day nurseries run by African American professionals and social service agencies. The African American day nurseries understood employment as an inevitable aspect of life, not as problematic or temporary. Acknowledging the long history of African American women's laboring as well as the exploitive conditions they often worked under, African American philanthropic societies responded benevolently to high rates of maternal wage-earning by providing full-time child care designed specifically to support employed mothers (Michel 1999).

In contrast, White-run day nurseries provided part-time child care in order to teach poor women and new immigrant mothers basic living skills, such as food preparation, hygiene, and parenting (Steinfels 1973). Poor mothers were aware that the middle-class women who ran the day nurseries disapproved of maternal employment, and they avoided using their childcare services unless absolutely necessary (Michel 1999). The association of group care with charity and the class biases of the middle-class women who ran these centers made even the poor working mothers who were eligible to use them dislike and distrust them.

Because group care originated in philanthropic efforts to rescue and reeducate poor women, childcare centers have been stigmatized by their association with poverty and family disintegration (Michel 1999). The stigma attached to center care was reinforced during the 1960s and 1970s when Head Start childcare centers were established by the government as part of the War on Poverty (Wrigley 1990). Middle-class, employed mothers avoided using childcare centers because they believed that centers were not intended for children from families like theirs—White, two-parent households living above the poverty line.

From the 1950s on, even as maternal employment increased, parents were steered away from center-based care by warnings about the dangers of institutional forms of care. The World Health Organization popularized British psychiatrist John Bowlby's theory that children who were not given opportunities to become attached to a mother figure would grow up to be adults unable to form close relationships with others (Bowlby 1951). Even though his research on maternal deprivation was based on children in orphanages and hospitals, the popular response was to view any nonmaternal care, including in childcare centers, as detrimental to children.

At the same time, however, the emerging scientific field of child development premised upon the notion that "most conscientious mothers could not expect to do a good job of raising children without expert help" (Wrigley 1990, 298) encouraged the use of childcare centers. Preschools and kindergartens first emerged in the 1920s to serve middle-class families by providing part-time enrichment programs to stimulate children's development and parent education for stay-at-home mothers (Joffe 1977; Wrigley 1990).

Recently, concerns that separation because of maternal employment might harm children have been laid to rest. A recent National Institute of Child Health and Development (NICHD) replication of the Ainsworth Strange Situation Task with children who had early childcare experiences (NICHD 1997) found that the amount of nonmaternal care and the child's age when the mother started employment were not related to the security of attachment relationship. Furthermore, the NICHD found "no direct effects of child care, either time of entry, amount of care, quality, stability or type of care, on infant-mother attachment" (NICHD 1997). Rather, maternal sensitivity and psychological adjustment were the significant predictors of infant attachment. Child care did play a role in interaction with maternal behaviors, in that poor quality care, significant amounts of care, and unstable care situations all appeared to increase the negative effects of low maternal responsiveness on child attachment (Hoffman and Youngblade 1999, 260–261). However, the NICHD study found that maternal employment does not directly affect the mother-child bond. If mothers are warm and responsive, infants are able to become securely attached, even if mothers are employed and children spend extended amounts of time in nonparental childcare arrangements. Other studies have found that maternal employment positively fosters independence and autonomy in girls (Hoffman and Youngblade 1999) and decreases problem behaviors by improving home environments (Haas 1999); in particular, poor children from at-risk backgrounds benefit from spending time in high-quality childcare settings (Hoffman and Youngblade 1999).

In all, the proposed benefits of enrichment opportunities for children offered by center-based child care has reconceived time spent in these centers as beneficial for children. These benefits outweigh doubts about whether children should be outside their mother's direct care. The rising acceptance of maternal employment and the growing legitimacy of these forms of child care contribute to the shift toward market-based childcare arrangements. It is less objectionable for families to use child care, including market-based services, when it is viewed as a privately determined choice made by individual families.

Dual Powerlessness

The political economy of the childcare market, which privatizes the care and devalues the labor, and the outdated ideological context, which questions mothers who transfer the care of their children to others, combine with the structural organization of daily care to complicate matters, because neither childcare providers nor mothers feel they have much power in the arrangement. The structural conditions leave both mothers and childcare providers feeling at risk. Margaret Nelson's book (1990) on family childcare providers first captured these dynamics:

> In their discussions of these complex relationships, each woman speaks as if she were the powerless one. Providers say they feel dependent on the willingness of parents to follow their rules. They note that because of the low prestige accorded child care they have few mechanisms to ensure compliance. They know that they are vulnerable to complaints lodged with state officials. They feel trapped, by their inability to assert themselves and by their awareness of the lack of alternatives, into continuing to offer care for children when they receive little financial reimbursement.

> And they feel captive to their own homes. Mothers speak of their extreme dependence on the provider they have found after an enervating search. They know that some providers disapprove of them, and they bristle at the suggestion that they are not being good mothers. They resent having to comply with rules that do not meet their needs. They feel vulnerable because they have so much at stake. And they question whether they have enough information to evaluate the situation. (79)

Neither providers nor mothers in this study felt that their role automatically granted them the upper hand in the relationship, or even a legitimate basis for expressing their concerns to the other.

The difficulty of finding a more acceptable arrangement prevented many mothers from asserting themselves. Mary Turner's sense of entitlement to question the care her child received was limited by her inability to pay more for better care. She said:

> That was my circumstance. I had been brought up middle class, and I was downwardly mobile. I had no right to criticize [the family childcare provider] unless she was doing something harmful. And if I wanted something better I had to pay more.

The consequence of these structural conditions of the market is that both parties were left feeling that they were held hostage in their current childcare arrangements.

Gwendolyn Jackson observed class differences in how the parents in her first childcare center and those in her second, more expensive center viewed their childcare situations. The middle-class parents in the second childcare center "were in the director's office all the time," whereas the working-class parents in the first childcare center did not ask for changes, and the director was often unavailable because she was solving other problems or covering staffing gaps in the childcare rooms. Gwendolyn thought that her ability to ask for what she wanted was related to her class status not only because of who she was but also because the childcare providers in the center perceived her as having authority because she was a professional. She said:

> Well, I'm sure it's a class issue. Most of them know what I do for a living. You go in there with a suit on every other day, they listen to you a little bit more closely. . . . It was very funny, because . . . I never tell people, I'm

> Dr. so and so, never do. . . . I don't put it on my application or nothing. Because I don't think it should matter on how you treat me nor my child. But one of my patients went and applied for a position there, and said, well, Dr. Gwendolyn Jackson sent me. They said, who is Dr. Gwendolyn Jackson? Ehhh, Niki's mom. She's a doctor? And when I came back that day . . . the whole rapport with me changed. They were trying to just meet my every need. And that ticked me off, because they should have been that way regardless.

She concluded that the tiered structure of the childcare market translates into different experiences according to the class of the parent and his or her sense of authority or disentitlement.

Individual characteristics of mothers and childcare providers played into this sense of uncertainty. Aurelia Fernandez, a Mexican immigrant childcare provider, was aware of how her ethnicity and immigrant background demoted her status. She reported that some White parents treated her disrespectfully:

> This one [White mother] . . . was prejudiced toward my race. . . . The way she used to talk to me. She'd just get, you know, look at me like I was down here and she was way up high. . . . And sometimes she would go, pssst, "Excuse me, I didn't understand that," and I would repeat and she would go, "Excuse me," and I would go, come on, lady, I know I have an accent, I admit to that, I mean, it's real heavy, but the kids can understand so I'm sure I am able to speak clearly for you, too. So I just got these vibrations, you know, real, that I didn't feel comfortable.

Had she been an assistant instead of the owner of her own family childcare business, Aurelia would have had to just accept this treatment. As the owner, however, Aurelia was able to exercise proprietary authority over the racial privilege of the Anglo American mother and asked the mother to find another place for her child.

It was very difficult for a family childcare provider to request that a family find other arrangements, because she wondered whether and when she would be able to find a replacement family in a precarious childcare economy. The risk of losing a family, whether because the provider decides to raise her rates or because of a conflict with the mother, is a constant threat that puts pressure on childcare providers to put up with a lot, even situations that make them uncomfortable, and to continue working with children and families they do not especially like.

Both structurally and interpersonally, mothers and childcare providers are unclear about who has the authority in the childcare relationship.

Rendering Maternal Employment Invisible

When a formal market of childcare services emerged in the 1980s, it provided some hope that the childcare needs of employed parents would be publicly recognized and addressed. For-profit childcare centers emerged as big business, corporations received tax incentives from the government to include childcare centers in their new buildings, and full-day care became the norm rather than a special add-on to enrichment programs. U.S. society had turned a corner, from viewing nonmaternal care as deviant to accepting the reality of dual-earner families and single working mothers, and acknowledging that very young children could benefit from exposure to adults outside their own families. Although a wide variety of childcare services is now readily purchasable and acceptable, there is still no workable childcare policy for working- and middle-class parents.

Mothers' doubts and worries flow from the structural conditions that privatize the process of selecting and maintaining childcare arrangements, regardless of local support for maternal employment and the development of childcare options. Their worries reflect not only their unconscious awareness of all the social ideas that shape the context within which they make their childcare arrangements but also conscious concerns about how to navigate interpersonal relationships with others when the principles of the relationships (market or care) are not clear.

Several social forces—the decreasing availability of women for care through familiar networks, the failure of public policy to acknowledge the childcare needs of employed mothers, the growing acceptability of maternal employment, the acceptance of nonmaternal care, and the perceived benefits of children spending time in child care—have contributed to the increased use of a market-based system of childcare services and the shift away from family-based and neighborhood-based care. Even though mothers still prefer loving, personal care for young children, center-based care is viewed more positively, whereas care by untrained providers in informal settings without expert supervision is viewed less favorably.

In the context of these changing conditions, several competing social ideas make it extremely difficult for mothers to define their expectations clearly and relinquish the care of their children to others without doubts and worries. First, remnants of the traditional ideology of domestic motherhood remain, and when mothers have doubts about the quality of their care, they also doubt whether they are doing the right thing even to have their children in nonparental care. Second, there are questions about how caring relationships, such as child rearing, can be transformed into market-based relationships: can anyone ever really be hired to "love" their child? Third, although families can easily find child care and leave their children with others, mothers know that they are responsible—and solely responsible—for monitoring that care. The lack of governmental regulations as well as the way in which these new services bring people of very different values and childrearing practices into association means that there is much uncertainty about whether that care fits with the family's ideas of child rearing. Finally, parents are aware that children and childcare providers spend long hours together, and the (possibly conflicting) needs of many, not just their own child, have to be taken into account. For example, a young child might need individual attention from a provider who is responsible for several children at once, or the need to provide constant supervision makes it difficult for the provider to do something as simple as go to the bathroom. So though parents want to be humane about their provider's needs, their young child's needs and well-being are their top priority, making it hard for parents to be confident consumers in the childcare market.

I opened this chapter with the question: How did this knotty state of affairs get formed? In the context of competing ideologies of motherhood, opportunities for employment, economic and social constraints, and value differences, it is not surprising that it is difficult to maintain a concern-free, or "perfect," childcare arrangement. Mothers appear to be behaving strangely, dodging their concerns, and government continues to take a hands-off approach and downplay the seriousness of the childcare needs of employed families. These conditions shift the responsibility for finding strategies to cope to the individual families, requiring mothers to establish ways to ensure the quality of care by themselves. The particularities of individual family childrearing practices and values, combined with the structural conditions of the organization of the work, regulatory neglect, and mothering ideologies, create a volatile mixture—one whose only predictable outcome is confusion, worry, and doubt for individual parents left on their own to navigate different childcare political economies.

Four

Transforming Arrangements into Relationships

Childcare arrangements are the sum of complex human relationships that bring an array of people into contact with one another on a daily basis. Many different relationships form the basis of this whole system of care, including relationships between childcare providers and children, parents and their children's caregivers, children and other children in care, and families and other families—that is, the community of people who share the same childcare situation. Such arrangements are fragile and volatile, yet at the same time they have the potential to develop into strong and stabilizing bonds among a variety of people. Bringing care-based relationships into market-based settings contributes to the instability, given that caring relationships assume commitment and attachment, but market relationships assume independence and free agency.

The relationship between the mother and the childcare provider is the primary adult relationship that oversees the quality of care the child receives from the care provider. There has not yet been much public discussion of the social experience of transferring one's children to paid caregivers. Instead, informal discussions among mothers themselves and emergent practices that are worked out between individual mothers and childcare providers give some definition to this situation. No established public "scripts" or social templates prescribe how this relationship should be conducted, and clear definitions of the roles of each party are not in place.

This is not an easy process to begin with, and the mix of market principles and care principles further confuse what the "rules of the game" are. Thus, the relationship is particularly changeable. The contradictory principles create confusion, and the societal assumption of private responsibility for parenting leaves it up to mothers and childcare providers to define their own practices.

One of the ways that mothers respond to their worries about the quality of child care is in how they define their relationships with their childcare providers. The definition of the nature of the relationship helps them manage their worries and give the process some clarity. Their definitions slip between market and care principles, however, as they selectively use the two sets of principles to define the relationship.

The lack of common understandings has led to the development of several different types of relationships between parents and childcare providers in order to make care work. Their views about the character of these relationships reflect the context of mixed market and care principles. Some mothers viewed them as formalized employer-employee and client-server relationships, while others established interpersonal relationships similar to friendships and even neighborhood-like communities in the childcare setting. Most commonly, mothers conceived of their relationships with their providers as childrearing partnerships. These relationships were important because they supported the parenting work of young families and helped them manage their worries about having their children in the care of others.

From the mothers I interviewed, I learned that interpersonal relationships with childcare providers formed an important foundation for daily management of childcare arrangements. Since mothers did not relinquish their responsibility for their children, the childcare provider was not only a substitute for what the mother would be doing, he or she was also a source of information about the child's daily well-being. The relationship between the mother and the childcare provider was critical to this communication.

Being an Employed Mother

Employed mothers cannot follow the traditional ideal of the mother who is constantly available in her young children's daily lives, providing a maternal presence and assuming responsibility for her child's social development. Maternal presence provides constant oversight that allows for a hands-on, attentive style of care that is responsive to immediate needs. When mothers place their children in childcare arrangements, this maternal ideal is not achievable, and mothering has to take place during more constricted periods of time, such as after work and on the weekends; when children are shifted to childcare providers, many mothering activities go with the child and become part of what the provider does. Mothers quickly learn that one of the most important relationships in their childcare arrangements is the relationship between themselves and their childcare providers.

Many studies have examined how mothers combine work and family, focusing on how housekeeping and parenting are redistributed between spouses. The assumption that many housekeeping and parenting responsibilities would be fairly equally shared by both partners has only been partially born out in practice. Most of the research shows that instead of shifting the load to partners, women are more likely to reduce overall what gets accomplished for the household and family members. Families eat out more instead of having home-cooked meals; beds do not get made every morning.

Mothers use time-management strategies to reduce the objective load, as well as the competing demands of these two sets of responsibilities. The list of strategies employed mothers use includes working part-time, intermittently, or on a flex-time basis; reducing housework time; compartmentalizing work and family in order to avoid time conflicts; cutting back on sleep; sequencing employment and child rearing; hiring domestic help and purchasing fast foods; and calling on spouses for more help at home (Haas 1999). These personal strategies do not challenge the assumption that employment and family are two separate spheres, but only reduce the ways they conflict with one another.

Combining work and family has also required employed mothers to develop image management strategies, or "strategies of being" (Garey 1999, 23) that allow them to reconcile contradictory roles and reconceptualize what it means to be an employed mother. Some of these strategies affirm, while others challenge, the traditional ideology of domestic motherhood. Gender strategies, such as the egalitarian, traditional, and transitional ideologies of marital roles described by Arlie Hochschild with Anne Machung (1989) in *The Second Shift,* not only define an employed mother's orientation to both work and family but also redefine her expectations of her partner's involvement in the home and the degree to which she is willing to share domestic responsibilities with her partner. The gender ideologies each couple develop allow them to reconcile the contradictions between their beliefs and the reality of how their lives are organized in practice.

Another way that mothers reframe the negative meaning of maternal employment is to reconceptualize paid work as part of mothering. Mothers often report that their children benefit from their economic contribution to the family, since it allows for higher standards of living, additional material advantages, and money for the extras that would not have otherwise been provided (Garey 1999). This economic dimension of motherhood makes mothers' employment a legitimate activity, rather than an activity in opposition to motherhood. Beatriz Pesquera (1985) found that employed Chicana mothers altered their ideas to resolve the contradiction between the cultural and the economic demands made on them as women; they redefined wage earning as part of motherhood because it benefited their families. Similarly, in her study of Mexican American and Mexican immigrant employed mothers, Denise Segura found that some mothers who were not ambivalent about being employed developed an ideology that employment is part of motherhood rather than in opposition to it, and they conceived of their employment as a way "to provide for their family's economic subsistence or betterment" (Segura 1994, 223). Chicano culture, like Anglo Protestant culture, has a dominant ideology of mothering "as the central element in the family and as the most important function and source of identity for Chicana women" (Pesquera 1985, 12). Under the traditional Chicano model of familism, women fulfill their mothering role through activities within the home, and outside activities are perceived as competing interests. Yet, in these cases, the meaning of motherhood is transformed to include paid work.

Employed mothers also reduce the apparent contradictions between the world of work and the world of family by fulfilling as much as possible both the image and the practices of stay-at-home motherhood. Some mothers manage this by bracketing their employment so that its visible impact on the family is unnoticeable to the rest of the family. In her study of employed mothers working in a hospital, Anita Garey (1995) found that several nurses worked nights so that they were available during the day; they appeared to others like full-time, stay-at-home mothers, even though they were functioning on less sleep.

Garey (1999) also found that employed mothers practiced symbolic acts of mothering in order to show that they were mothering even if they did not stay at home. For example, the mother who takes time off from her job to go on a field trip is more of a "real mother" than her co-worker who never goes on field trips. (Whether stay-at-home mothers chaperone field trips is irrelevant, since the nonemployed mother does not need to affirm her commitment to or status as a "real mother" symbolically.) Employed mothers also affirm their motherhood by breast feeding, actively engaging in "family time," such as ensuring that their families sit down for meals together, or doing school-related activities, such as helping with homework, volunteering in their children's classrooms, and transporting children to extracurricular activities. Other mothering activities, such as counting developmental milestones (such as being the one who sees the "first baby step"), are counted only when the mother first sees them in order to affirm the mother's status in spite of her regular, employment-related absences.

Rethinking Quality Time

Another approach some employed mothers use to preserve their identities as traditional mothers is to consider "quality time" an acceptable substitute for the "quantity time" that stay-at-home mothers spend with their children. Sharon Hays (1996) found that employed mothers who believed in the contemporary cultural model of appropriate mothering based on labor-intensive, child-centered, expert-guided child rearing continued to adhere to this model by compressing their mothering activities into fewer hours in order to accomplish all the traditional expectations of motherhood. Some employed mothers believe that they are good mothers because they spend higher-quality time focusing on their children than results from the less interactive presence of nonemployed mothers who are available to their children full-time. As long as mothers can spend bursts of high-quality family time with their children and organize their children's lives successfully, then their mothering responsibilities are not compromised by their lengthy absences. By rearticulating motherhood on the basis of the nature of the time that they spend with their children, rather than on how much time overall they spend together, mothers also mask changes in the way they mother. Yet, "one might also point out the sense of guilt regarding unfulfilled obligations that this notion [of quality time] implies and the sense of emotional commitment and moral obligation that is hidden just beneath the surface" (Hays 1996, 160–161). The notion of "quality time" is an image management strategy to render invisible their reduced presence and enhance their status as mothers.

This new ideology of "quality time" changes how employed mothers interact with their children when they are with them. One of the major differences between the "quality time" that employed mothers provide and "quality time" that nonemployed mothers give is that quality time for employed mothers is labor-intensive in compact periods of time. Ongoing constant presence and availability are replaced with focused attentiveness and interaction, as well as purposefully planned, structured activities. This contrasts with the type of time—"being there," "hanging out," or "availability" (see Lamb, Pleck, and Charnov 1985)—that stay-at-home mothers can provide for their children. Because the content of interaction shifts from "being there" to "doing things together," it narrows interactions to more highly organized activities, which for middle-class families can become very expensive (such as going out to eat together instead of using the time to cook a meal, purchasing admissions to sources of family entertainment, such as movies, fairs, children's museums, and play parks). Employed mothers use this logic of "intensive mothering" (Hays 1996) or "intentional parenting" (Galinsky 1999) to counter any negative self-evaluations that they are neglectful, inattentive, or absent mothers. Ellen Galinsky found that children of employed mothers also seemed to be less concerned about the amount of time that their mothers spent with them, and more aware of the quality of that time. Children objected to their parents' employment-related absences only when stresses and bad moods from work interfered with the time children were with their parents (1999, 49).

On the surface, this notion of "quality time" may appear to be a time-management strategy: that is, mothering responsibilities are compressed into shorter periods of time. However, the act of compressing mothering into short periods of time also transforms the definition of what constitutes mothering and how it is accomplished. The concept of "quality time" eliminates the assumption that mothers are supposed to be present all the time in order to be good mothers. Whether this idea truly challenges the notion that employment undermines motherhood is not entirely clear, but the practice allows mothers to feel that they are fulfilling both work and family responsibilities. Mothering shifts into the realm of management rather than requiring that mothers carry out specific mothering tasks and activities themselves.

Transferring Mother Work to Others

Mothers also preserve their mothering identities by viewing what childcare providers do as not substituting for motherhood even when they shift childrearing activities to other people. By dividing childrearing activities that have traditionally been combined under the rubric of motherhood into components and delegating some of them to others, mothers can share childrearing activities with childcare providers without feeling that their mothering is being diminished (Hertz and Ferguson 1996). Cameron Macdonald found that employed mothers who hired in-home caregivers, such as nannies, au pairs, and immigrant women, "reinforce a particular idealized version of motherhood, and simultaneously obscure the underlying reality of the practice of shared mother-work" (1998, 27). Macdonald discovered in her interviews with mothers who hired in-home nannies that the nannies' work was rendered invisible in order to maintain the mother's status as the child's primary caretaker. Together, mothers and nannies created informal rules that hid the real division of mother work and reinforced the mother's place and identity as the primary caregiver in the traditional sense of domestic motherhood. For example, they defined a clear end of the nanny's workday in order to create a sharp boundary between family time and nanny time in order to minimize the acknowledgment of nanny-child bonds. Mothers wanted nannies who would be an "extension of themselves who would stay home as if she were the mother, but who would vanish upon the real mother's return, leaving no trace of her presence in the psychic lives of the children they shared" (Macdonald 1998, 34). By calling what they did "shadow work," nannies colluded with their employers. Acknowledging that their emotional connections with the children in their care can only be temporary, they practiced the same kind of detached attachment that Margaret Nelson (1990) found among experienced family childcare providers.

Depending on which ideology of motherhood mothers espoused, families and mothers held different expectations of their childcare providers (Uttal 1996a; Hertz 1997). Some families felt that mothers were the people primarily responsible for the children's upbringing, and they organized child care so that it maintained an ideal view of family life organized around mother care, even when care was transferred to others (Hertz 1997). If families believed that child rearing could only be the product of a dyadic relationship and they sought to maintain the mother's identity as the child's primary caregiver, they viewed children's time in care as strictly custodial, even if it exceeded thirty hours a week and even if, in practice, childcare providers were "mothering" the children in their care. However, if mothers acknowledged how much child rearing the provider was doing, they viewed the care as surrogate; they believed that they could be replaced by the childcare provider as the primary caregiver, who functioned as the child's mother in the traditional sense of child rearing (Uttal 1996a).

I found a third model for the roles of mother and provider among the mothers I interviewed. When mothers did not adhere to the notion that a child is mothered solely or primarily by one person, they believed that multiple adults could carry out the activities of mothering, and they viewed what childcare providers did with their children as a form of co-parenting that did not undermine their status as the child's mother. When this understanding prevailed, mothers discussed and coordinated their care with the provider, though they did so to varying degrees. There was an important limit to this sharing of care, however. Children could have several primary caregivers who cared for them on a regular basis, but they could only have one mother who had executive responsibility for their long-term well-being.

The time- and image-management strategies that employed mothers use, such as rendering employment invisible, delegating housework to others, and preserving their identity and status as domestic mothers, do not work when mothers are trying to define the delegation of maternal care to others and to justify separating a child from his or her mother for extended periods of time. Even though mothers may try to hide their employment or deny the market basis of the care work that their childcare providers do by dressing it up as family-like, the reality is that they are involving other adults in carrying out child rearing. Unlike housework that can be left undone, or partners whose absence from household management can be ignored, good mothering requires active involvement and interaction with all of the adults who are providing care for the child in the mother's absence.

Family Metaphors

Many mothers used family terms to describe their relationships with their childcare providers. They often referred to their childcare provider as "like a second mother" or "just like family" to their children. Donna Weissman said, "I consider babysitters a part of our family . . . if they take care of your children they're very much a part of your family." Stephanie Harris said, "Miss Myrtle was like, almost like family . . . like a grandmother." Bonnie Taylor said of her in-home childcare provider, "I want a person I can treat like my family and is willing to treat my children like their family. That's what I want." Even when mothers used institutional care, they used family metaphors frequently to describe both the relationship between the child and the childcare provider and that between mother and childcare provider. Mary Turner said, "I try to establish like a family relationship with the caregivers and really get to know them very well." Gwen Kennedy said about the childcare center where her child went, "We like the contact with the staff. It's a real family feeling there which is really good for us. . . . And that had been like a family. [Our daughter] loved . . . we loved one of her afternoon caregivers." Some mothers said that they related to the childcare provider "as if she were my own mother" or "like a sister to me."

Some mothers metaphorically described their childcare arrangements as their extended families. Lucinda Curtis and her husband, Jim, were computer consultants who telecommuted from their home. They relied on a group of young college women to care for their two-year-old son, Zachary, for thirty hours a week. Gretchen, a young woman in her mid-twenties, had started providing care for Zachary when he was three months old. As Gretchen became less available, she brought in her friends as additional sources of child care. Lucinda described this group of childcare providers: "[Jim and I] joke that we have purchased an extended family. We live in a capitalist society [and we are] a nuclear family without grandparents, without family whatsoever. So we purchase extended family. That's what we do." Lucinda's comment captures the ironic synthesis of family and money in childcare arrangements.

Yet, when most mothers used these family metaphors, they masked how childcare arrangements are fundamentally based on the payment for labor and were usually short-term. This figure of speech obscured the fact that parents have the ultimate authority to decide when to terminate the arrangement that brought the caring relationship into existence. Childcare providers similarly, though less frequently, described themselves as "like their family" or "a grandmother to her" (Murray 1998; Nelson 1990). However, childcare providers were fully aware that while they may behave "like moms," they remained outside the "dominant cultural ideology of what constitutes family [and] currently acceptable models of motherhood" (Murray 1998, 149).

The language of family-like relationships was limited in its applicability because, in fact, neither mothers nor childcare providers expected or gave as much as family relationships assume. Although mothers often use the language of family to describe these relationships, there were things that they still would not be comfortable with nonfamily members doing. Vanessa Grey would let her brother pick up her child and bring her home, but she would not accept the same offer from her childcare provider. She assumed that families can be called upon to meet certain needs and can be trusted to carry out those responsibilities, whereas it was inappropriate and unwise for childcare providers to be entrusted with them; kinship implied both long-term caring and personal responsibility, whereas child care was limited to specific times and tasks. Where the boundaries were actually drawn varies from mother to mother, yet the acknowledgement of distinction between a family member and a childcare provider was always made.

At the same time that the family metaphor was used, paid childcare relationships were understood to be short term in comparison to family relationships. The relationship between the child and provider did not involve the same permanent connection and sense of lastingness that family relationships entailed. Even though the care of young children demands emotional attention, this connection existed only as long as the service relationship existed. Although childcare providers may genuinely care for a child, the existence of their caring relationship was premised upon having been hired to perform a service. Payment changed hands. In fact, expectations of long-term attachments were problematic in this work because the childcare provider did not have the authority to ensure the continued existence of a relationship with any of the children she has been hired to care for. Although the bond between child and provider was often defined and authentically experienced as a caring relationship, the relationship's existence depended on functional need for services. Even though care was organized as a family-like relationship, it was still fundamentally a purchased service.

Family metaphors were used to deal with the ambiguity and contradictions that exist when the prevailing ideology that private families are supposed to raise their own children was juxtaposed with the actual practice of hiring nonfamily members to share child rearing. The family euphemism obscures the business basis of childcare work, yet it did not propose or clarify what kinds of relationship should have been or were established between mother and provider.

Defining Different Relationships

Mothers articulated different types of relationships that they established with their childcare providers, drawing simultaneously on the metaphoric language of family and the market-based language of a service economy. These definitions of the relationship reduced some of the ambiguity of who was doing what and clarified expectations between mother and childcare provider.

Keeping It Businesslike

Some mothers spoke about their relationships as if they were employer-employee or client-server relationships. Cordial but professional interactions kept the relationship within the boundaries of a service provided in exchange for payment and kept other social expectations in check. Like the parents in Wrigley's (1995) study, some mothers maximized the social distance between themselves and their providers. When child care was narrowly conceived as a formal service, mothers had clearly delimited expectations of what it was supposed to provide and how it was supposed to work as a business arrangement. At the time I interviewed them, eleven of the forty-eight employed mothers in this study maintained a businesslike relationship with their childcare providers. For these parents, a childcare arrangement was a service, rather than an interpersonal relationship, both for their children and for themselves.

Three of these eleven mothers articulated their childcare arrangements in ways that seemed especially service-based. They prioritized adult-centered needs in discussions of their childcare arrangements. They emphasized such functional factors as convenience, cost, hours of availability, closed days, and the logistics of getting children to and from care, rather than the childcare provider's relationship with their child or themselves. Although these mothers had chosen their childcare arrangement based on criteria that included what the child needed, their concerns about maintaining it revolved around how well it was working for them. These three mothers did not know about the actual content of their child's daily care; they could reiterate the criteria that they originally used to choose the care, such as the formal opportunities that were provided to their children, the daily schedules described in the parent handbook, and the amenities of the physical environment, but their words did not convey that they had any more knowledge about the childcare arrangement than what they had originally observed when choosing the care. Nothing they said pertained to those qualities that characterize developing or ongoing interpersonal relationships.

Adult priorities were evident when mothers had to weigh the quality of child care against its functional advantages. Although Brenda Sharpe complained about the lack of communication with her childcare providers, she maintained the arrangement because it was convenient. When I asked if she had thought about changing her childcare arrangement, she first responded that she did not have time to look for a new arrangement. Then she admitted, self-critically:

> But I sure make time for two softball teams. So, you know, there is time. And, I've taken long lunches before from work. I could do it. But, I guess, change, the idea of changing again. It's all selfish reasons, I think. As much as I love my baby, I don't want to drive ten miles out of my way. I mean, I'm being perfectly honest with you. . . . I've said things that I would never tell other people. I'm just telling you the truth, like I don't want to drive ten miles.

In other words, she saw child care as a service that could not be transformed, and she knew that she was unwilling to request changes because she was not willing to change her arrangements to get what she wanted. And in deciding whether to change for something better, or stay put because it was convenient, she prioritized her own needs over those of her child. Though Brenda doubted the care and questioned whether it was working the way she wanted it to, she sidestepped her concerns by defining her child care as a purchased service that gave her what it was supposed to; thus, she found it acceptable. The concerns that she had were not valid according to this definition and could be dismissed, or, at least, prioritized below her adult needs.

Treating child care as a service that catered primarily to the mother's employment-related needs was the least common understanding of business-like childcare arrangements, however. Eight of the eleven mothers who viewed child care as a service also talked about the opportunities it offered their children. These mothers continued to keep tabs on the content of their child's daily care, even though they maintained their own social distance from the provider. In these cases, mothers asked about how the child's day had gone, what the child had eaten, how the child had slept, and what activities the child might have participated in. They did not articulate any expectation that their childcare arrangement should provide them with social connections or support, even in parenting.

By viewing child care as a service, mothers garnered a sense of confidence in their childcare providers. These mothers were not inattentive to the quality of care their child was receiving; instead, they felt that the autonomy they gave their providers recognized them as knowledgeable, competent workers. Autonomy gave the childcare provider the authority to define and manage the child care in the mother's absence. For example, Donna Weissman, a White, middle-class mother, hired an elderly African American woman to keep house and care for her children until they were each eighteen months old. Other than making it clear that the care of her children took priority over the housecleaning, Donna never instructed her provider what to do. Donna explained that she let the provider make her own decisions because she trusted her based on her years of experience, and Donna also did not want her to feel criticized or mistrusted. Donna was aware of differences between her own practices and the provider's, but she respectfully accepted the way her provider cared for her children while they were infants and toddlers.

Instead of being perturbed by differences, Donna found humor in some of them. For example, Donna returned home from work one day to find her White daughter's hair filled with multiple braids, beads, and ties in a style commonly given to African American children. Donna removed the beads and ties as soon as her provider left, yet she never told her childcare provider that she did not want her daughter's hair styled that way. Instead,

Donna turned a blind eye to what she defined as small differences in styles of caregiving because this approach allowed her to create a respectful relationship out of the servant tradition of hiring African American housekeepers that she had inherited from her own parents.

By granting her childcare provider full authority, she was also attempting to turn the structurally hierarchical and racialized employer-employee relationship between White middle-class employers and lower-status African American housekeepers into a respectful, client-service provider relationship. Treating her provider with respect took priority, regardless of their cultural and class differences. Since this care was confined to Donna's private home, the African American hairstyles and color combinations that her provider applied to her child and Donna found strange were not problematic. Donna's definition of her childcare provider's responsibility was to "mind the baby." She was comfortable with the care her child received and felt the provider was doing her job well. The provider clearly provided a safe environment, and watched over, fed, and interacted with the child in a responsible way. This was the service that Donna expected and Donna felt that maintaining a respectful employer-employee relationship ensured that her provider would continue to give her child quality attention.

Another reason that some mothers characterized their relationships as strictly business was when they wanted to create boundaries between themselves and their childcare providers. By amplifying the business aspects of paid care, mothers were able to create some temporary distance between themselves and their providers. This withdrawal occurred when mothers were worried about their childcare arrangements but had not yet decided to speak with the provider about their concerns. Even if their relationships had been more personal, the temporary cooling inherent in defining child care as a service allowed them to detach from the interpersonal relationship in order to see the quality of care more clearly. When Aurora Garcia had serious doubts about the quality of her long-term childcare arrangement with a family childcare provider whom she had come to feel was part of her family, she needed this distance from their personal relationship to evaluate the quality of the care. She felt obligated to the provider as someone who had established a long-term relationship with her child, as well as with her. She was worried about the economic impact on the provider of withdrawing her child from care, as well as about the lack of respect indicated by her doubting the provider's ability to deliver quality care. In order to downplay these interpersonal concerns, she temporarily made her relationship with the provider more businesslike.

Mothers also became more businesslike after they had decided to terminate an arrangement and were looking for a new one. Some mothers became very formal in order to accelerate the process of disengagement. By emphasizing the market relationship, mothers minimized the significance of the emotional bonds between provider and child (Macdonald 1998) as well as between the mother and provider (Wrigley 1995). For example, Kathryn Ercolini discounted the significance of personal relationships when she decided to terminate her childcare arrangement when the family childcare provider raised her rates. She spoke with great respect about the provider and was not dissatisfied with the content of the care, but she did not want to pay more for the service, believing she could find new arrangements at the old rate. Even though she was very satisfied with this family childcare provider, her orientation toward child care as primarily a service that should cost a certain amount led her to disregard the significance of her child's relationship with the provider, as well as the quality of her own relationship with her. Diminishing the emotional significance of a particular caregiver and viewing changing providers as acceptable for financial reasons heightens the characterization of the relationship as a businesslike one.

Defining the relationships in more businesslike terms also allowed mothers to move out of them gracefully. Whenever arrangements were being terminated because of dissatisfaction with the quality of care or interpersonal conflicts between mothers and childcare providers, both the mothers and childcare providers were uncomfortable. Since there was usually lag time between a decision to leave an arrangement and the establishment of a new one, the mother and the childcare provider still had to interact with one another. At this point, it was difficult for them to manage the personal connections and emotions involved in the situation. By narrowing the definition of the relationship to a business model, mothers could more easily justify their decision, especially when there was disagreement about the reasons for terminating the arrangement. If a mother could not procure the services that she wanted at the price she was willing to pay, it was her prerogative to seek out new services, and this made termination more palatable, even if there was a fondness between the mother and childcare provider. Childcare providers also said that if mothers were not satisfied, they should look for what they wanted elsewhere. Conceiving of the relationship as a business one made it easier to attribute the failure to consumer needs and market pressures, not failure in quality of care or personal connections. The definition of the relationship as a business arrangement also tempered the mother's guilt about interrupting an established relationship between her child and the childcare provider, as well as between herself and the childcare provider, because the logic of market pressures (such as cost, convenience of location) could be articulated and accepted as more important than the illusive logic of care (such as attachment).

Although these relationships were sometimes businesslike because new mothers did not know better, mothers often deliberately defined them as businesslike in order to manage their concerns about the quality of care and how to extricate themselves from them.

Befriending the Childcare Provider

A market-based arrangement between a mother and a childcare provider, even when they do not initially know one another, has the potential to personalize and, in its deepest form, become a friendship that continues even after the children no longer need care. Four of the forty-eight mothers described their relationship with their current childcare provider as a friendship. None of them had been acquainted prior to establishing their childcare arrangement. Their relationships had grown beyond the childcare services rendered to the family, beyond the paycheck paid to the provider, and even beyond the bond between the child and the provider. The regularity of daily contact and the fact that caring is a dynamic human relationship and not a commodity contributes to the personalization of the relationship. Just as it is unrealistic to believe that children who are in the care of others for thirty to sixty hours per week will not be socialized by childcare providers, it is also unrealistic to think that mothers and providers who see each on a daily basis and share the care of a child will not become familiar with one another. In these cases, the logic of care principles move to replace the logic of market principles upon which the relationship was originally established.

Intimacy and a sense of connection developed when mothers and providers extended their interactions beyond the care of the child. Conversations were no longer confined to talking about the children and often turned to other topics, furthering a sense of familiarity and a friendship bond. Cassie Lee Smith said:

> It's not all centered around Franny, and how her day was. It's just much more, on a friend basis. It really seems to be . . . more than a professional [one]. So, it's, we have lots of conversations, not about kids at all, which is really nice.

Christy Roundtree, Franny's childcare provider, also saw her relationship with Cassie Lee as a friendship. Christy often developed comradeships with the parents she worked for, even though most of them had been strangers prior to coming to her for child care. Christy said:

> I've been real lucky because I'm friends with all my parents. . . . I'm friends with all of them, so if we're not chatting about the babies, we're chatting about, "Well, did you, you know, do such and such last night" or, "Have you started painting your kitchen?" And, you know, so one way or the other, we're chatting about something.

Joyce Lewis described her close relationship with her childcare provider:

> I just walked in every day, and we hugged [and] we talked about everything. . . . I don't know what the reason is, that you connect with people, there's just something there, but that's the way I felt with Pauline. That there was something there. . . . We talked about everything . . . about my mother, or religions, or, everything, recipes, just everything. She was my friend.

The friendship between Laurie Seitz and Carol Prentice resembled many that develop between young mothers, especially in family childcare homes. Carol's name was on a list that Laurie received from a resource and referral service. Both were middle-class married White women with young children; they lived in similar neighborhoods. Their friendship first emerged from spending time together when Laurie picked up her child at the end of the day. Laurie would arrive after work and find a place on the carpet with

Carol and the children. While offering extra adult help to the kids, she talked with Carol about a wide range of topics. As most mothers do when they get together with their children, Carol and Laurie "multitasked." While they changed diapers and assisted children, the two of them would have adult conversations. Carol's family childcare home was a place for Laurie to relax after a day of work, and she often stayed for as long as an hour. While other mothers might have stayed each day because they were monitoring their child care, this was not the case for Laurie. Laurie did not have strong ideas about what she expected from child care. And as long as Laurie left before Carol had to get ready to receive other parents, Carol appreciated the adult companionship and extra pair of hands. Eventually, Carol and Laurie also socialized outside the childcare setting. Carol first invited Laurie to join her and another friend for a "girls' night out on the town." They also attended Bible study group together. Since then, they have regularly gone out together, sometimes double dating with their husbands.

Stephanie Harris and Tracy Lowry also became friends through their childcare arrangement. Stephanie was an administrative assistant and Tracy was a childcare worker in a for-profit childcare center. Like Laurie and Carol, Stephanie and Tracy were very similar to one another. Both were working-class young married African American women, though Tracy did not have any children yet. Stephanie explained how they became familiar with one another:

> We saw each other for years every day. You know, even though she wasn't [my child]'s teacher we just got to know each other. I don't know! I just like her and she liked me. I guess just a personality thing . . . she's still working [at the childcare center]. She was there before we got there; she'll probably be there forever. . . . And we got to be friends. . . . Like I say, you see a person every day. . . . You know, day after day you see these people; and she would always speak. She would comment about [my child] even before she was in her class, "Oh, she's so cute." And we just would chit-chat.

Like Laurie, Stephanie felt that the provider initiated the friendship by offering invitations to get together beyond the childcare setting. Stephanie explained:

> She invited me over to her house one day. . . . The husbands met, they liked each other, so she invited us to go out with them for New Year's, and we did. . . . [Other childcare providers] all would speak to you but she like held a conversation with me. I guess that's how you make friends anywhere; you meet them, and you talk to them and you see you have things in common, or whatever. . . . The more we talked we just saw we had a lot in common and we just liked each other. . . . As time went on we just try to think of things to do just on the social end.

Tracy's extended conversations with Stephanie initially created the foundation upon which a friendship was built. The establishment of friendships between the adults in the childcare arrangement shifted attention away from thinking of child care as strictly a business arrangement or a relationship that existed only through the child. Becoming friends required that the mother and childcare provider discovered shared interests, not only child-centered ones. Not surprisingly, shared social characteristics, as evident with Laurie and Carol and Stephanie and Tracy facilitated growth of friendships outside the childcare setting. These deeper connections cement a relationship between two women that is greater than the shared care of a child.

Childcare arrangements that developed into friendships allowed mothers to sidestep some of their worries about nonparental care. Implied by the mother and childcare provider's friendship was a commitment to take special care of the child, the kind that family or friends would give. The connection between the mother and the childcare provider was an additional assurance that the childcare provider would provide quality care, above and beyond the provider's own expertise, motivation, or commitment to children.

But when childcare providers and mothers were friends, they sometimes allowed their adult relationship to take priority over their concern for the children's needs. Conversations about their daily adult lives replaced conversations about how the child was doing in care, because it was assumed that this care was fine.

Familiarity can contribute to a greater sense of trust and less scrutiny of the care than may be warranted by the quality of care being provided by the childcare provider. Adult friendships may even explain why more parents do not report greater dissatisfaction with their situations or delay removing their children from substandard care. For example, Laurie Seitz hired a woman she befriended who lived in her neighborhood to care for her child. Because they were neighbors and knew each other prior to setting up the childcare arrangement, she assumed that the woman shared her ideas about child rearing. Laurie's overly trustful view of what kind of care the neighbor would provide impeded her initial assessment of how her child would be cared for. After the arrangement was established she discovered that the woman did not use the seatbelt when she put the child's car seat in the car and she did not handle basic health care concerns the same way Laurie would. Personal bonds delayed Laurie's decision.

Instead of being concerned first and foremost about what was in the child's best developmental interest, friendship-based relationships mimicked family relationships. When care was based on friendship, adult relationships also were key factors in how mothers assessed their satisfaction with the care. The criteria for determining satisfaction with care were different from those used to evaluate the quality of care, and this was especially evident when mothers felt connected to their childcare providers. The more familiar mothers were with their childcare providers, the less likely it was for mothers to raise their doubts for discussion. Familiarity could interfere with prioritizing child-centered needs or striving for better communication about a child's daily well-being, though familiarity did ease mothers' worries as long as the care was basically satisfactory. When concerns did arise, mothers hesitated to question their childcare providers because they felt constrained by their adult relationships. Mothers had to think much more carefully about the consequences of criticizing or rejecting a friend's care, even if it was in the child's best interest to do so, than about ending an arrangement with someone with whom they had maintained a businesslike relationship.

Establishing Childrearing Partnerships

Most of the mother-provider relationships were not maintained as strictly business arrangements, nor did they develop the intimacy of friendship. Sharing the care of a child is, in itself, a powerful basis of connection, especially when the mother chose the provider because she appreciated her values and liked the style of child care given. Thirty-five of the forty-eight mothers described their childcare relationships in a way that I conceptualized as "childrearing partnerships." These relationships were organized around and limited to a shared interest in the well-being of a particular child. Conversations about caring for the child occurred when mothers brought in their children or came to pick them up. Although these exchanges were often brief, they were regular, and over time they provided the foundation for a working partnership. Within such partnerships, mothers could seek advice about parenting issues and articulate their concerns.

At the start of a new childcare arrangement, conversations between mothers and providers enabled them to learn about, clarify, and get a bearing on one another's childrearing values and practices. For example, Jana Swift said:

> It was almost like we had a camaraderie. We were both women, we were both mothers, and we were both trying to make it and have a little bit of, you know, still have some kind of goodness in our lives or richness in our lives. She seemed, I mean, we're similar in the way that I felt that we both appreciated, we had the same kind of values, like what was real important [in the world] was not a lot of material things but more things like honesty and love and that, you know, those real basic kind of values rather than material values. . . . It just seemed like a given that we both agreed on these things. . . . I think it gave me a sense of security with her. She expected the same things of [my child] that I would expect of him. . . . Basically, she didn't approve of the same things I didn't approve of.

Denise Johnson reiterated these feelings when she described how she was comfortable with her childcare provider because she felt they shared the same values about child rearing. She described their similarities:

> Just the way she is, she doesn't spank her kids and she doesn't scream at them, she talks to them, she spends a lot of time with them. Like a lot of the problems I have had she's had like my son moved out of our bed when Tracy was born and now Tracy's in our bed and it's the same thing with her. . . . My son won't eat vegetables and her sons wouldn't eat vegetables so she fed them fruit . . . instead of arguing with them over it, and I feel the same way where my husband doesn't, where her husband didn't.

> I'm like just give them what you can rather than tying them down and shoving it down their throats, just kind of go with the flow, that's what I mean. She's got . . . basically the same kind of attitude about child rearing.

Just as doubts shook their confidence, discovering common values and sharing similar expectations facilitated mothers' confidence in their new childcare providers.

It was not necessary for values to be tightly shared as long as the relationship developed between the mother and childcare provider gave the mother a sense that she could work with the childcare provider in her child's best interest. Even mothers who were very socially different seemed to be able to create this trust with one another. When Sally Trainer first met Aurelia Fernandez, they appeared to have very little in common with one another. Sally was a White, single, never-married mother, who was self-confident and fast-moving. Aurelia was a Mexican immigrant woman, married and the mother of two children, who was soft-spoken, deeply religious, and traditional in her family values. Despite their differences, Sally sensed that she and Aurelia shared a strong commitment to the well-being of children. Sally chose Aurelia to care for her three-year-old daughter, Sophie, because she recognized that Aurelia's foundational values about child rearing fit with her own.

Every day when Sally picked up her daughter, she initiated conversations with Aurelia about how Sophie was doing. They talked about how her daughter was adjusting to the new childcare setting and how to handle such matters as the fact that Sophie was not taking naps there. Sally and Aurelia often discussed childrearing issues: how to guide children; how to handle time outs; how to let children draw outside the lines when they colored; how to respond to children's play when it had violent themes. These daily conversations were critical to Sally's continuing confidence in the care, especially in the early days of the new arrangement for her.

As Sophie settled into the situation, conversations between Aurelia and Sally shifted to new topics. They talked about Aurelia's children, and about how Aurelia had immigrated to the United States as a teenager. They talked more about how their own workdays went—Sally at the office, Aurelia in her home. These conversations helped them both let go of their work and return to being family-focused. Occasionally, Aurelia invited Sally to stay for dinner with her family. Although the two did not socialize together outside of Aurelia's family childcare home, their shared concern about child rearing was the anchor of their relationship. Childrearing partnerships remain focused on the shared care of a child within the childcare setting. Unlike friendship-based relationships, Sally and Aurelia kept the child central in their conversations. Their discussions made it easy for Sally to raise her concerns; her worries never turned into monsters, because she addressed them before that happened.

Childrearing partnerships, like that between Sally and Aurelia, also provided a means for crossing social differences and creating bonds. Mothers could accept differences in values and practices when they regarded them as beneficial to their child's social development. Mothers tolerated differences when they viewed them as offering enrichment opportunities for their children. For example, Gretchen Hall viewed the difference between her personality and that of her childcare provider as positive for her infant. She said:

> You know I actually think it is good that there are differences because you need a balance. I like how she is calm. I find that soothing. I find her sweet. . . . She probably doesn't have a loud sense of humor. . . . But I am pretty crazy, wild, and goofy when I play with Heidi. She probably plays with Heidi differently. . . . Heidi is very comfortable with her. Heidi likes her. And she knows how to talk to Heidi. And the way that she talks to Heidi makes her feel good. It soothes her. [L: Would you like someone like yourself taking care of Heidi during that childcare time?] No, because . . . I don't see myself as someone fit to stay at home. I feel there is something missing. While I see, well, I like the fact that there is a balance. She . . . augments in what she gives to her. It is just the quality of her nature. And I am just not into babies. I may be able to watch a friend's baby for a couple of hours but not day in day out.

In fact, Gretchen was appreciative that her childcare provider's personality was more suited to the kind of care that she felt infants should get than her own style would have been. Differences were acceptable as long as mothers could coordinate what happened in the childcare arrangement with home. Becky Mueller said:

> I think that what happens at preschool affects what happens at home; what happens at home affects what happens at preschool. And there has to be communication about those happenings. . . . Like wanting to know what's going on with my child. I'm not the kind of parent that can just drop off my kid and forget about him for four hours; and not care about what happened to him during that portion of his life. I'm not into controlling that portion of his life. But I'm into helping with the adjustment. And I need enough information so that I can talk to Sean for the rest of the day about what's going on, and I need to know that the teachers are also seeing . . . if there's a problem and that they're working on it. I need to know what they're doing and that they are doing something and progress reports.

When mothers saw the advantage of exposing their children to differences, it not only allayed their need to have nonmaternal care match maternal care, it also allowed them to prioritize their children's experiences above adult needs. For example, Gloria Thomas, an African American mother, was not at ease with the style of the predominantly middle-class and White childcare center where her child went. She was uncomfortable with her interactions with the childcare providers, whom she disparagingly described as "soft-spoken," "hippied out," and "being happy all the time," and with the other parents, who had more affluent and leisurely lives than was possible for her as a busy single parent. She said, "They are probably used to dealing with these other parents that are, you know, that have togetherness, aren't stressed out." Despite her own discomfort, Gloria kept her child in this center because she felt it offered superior educational opportunities.

Accepting differences facilitated childrearing partnerships between mothers and providers who were not similar. When mothers discovered that they did not share the same values or practices as their providers, they could bring maternal care into alignment with nonmaternal care by adopting the provider's practices. Some mothers changed their ways of doing things to mirror what the childcare provider was doing. Marci Washington originally did not want to stop bringing her son's bottle to his family childcare home, but when the childcare provider insisted, she decided to try out what the provider was recommending.

> I would bring the bottle with him, and she said, oh, no, no, no, we don't need that. And she said, I don't give it to him, when we're here, so she'd say I could take it back with me. . . . She really felt that, at his age, he was, and he was almost two, so I really should stop doing that. So, I think she was kind of, saying that, we don't need the bottle. I don't think she really gave it, she didn't, wouldn't, didn't give it to him while he was there. . . . So, then I decided, I said let's try, and I wanted to try her way, and so I would not take the bottle back [to child care], I wouldn't, just to see how he would do. And that was fine with me.

In the end, Marci appreciated that her son was weaned from his bottle. The experience of having successfully reached a mutual agreement about how to handle a difference also shored up her confidence in her childcare provider.

Successful childrearing partnerships hinge on open exchanges and mutual compromises made by mothers and providers. Early childhood educator Janet Gonzalez-Mena (2000) advises childcare providers to listen to and to learn from parents, especially when there are cross-cultural differences. Sometimes providers can teach parents new ways to do things, but childcare providers can also learn to understand why parents may be resistant or have different practices and can agree to adopt parental practices. A third possibility is that parents and providers, by learning from one another, can develop new practices that are not only in the child's best interest but also allow parents and providers to be comfortable with sharing the care of the same child and feel that they are coordinating their childrearing practices. As Cassie Lee Smith pointed out:

> Any downfalls that we feel [about]Christy, anything that we think Christy might not be doing, exactly like we would do it, she makes up for it in other ways. I have to say that, my only criticism would be nutrition there. I'm very picky about what Franny eats, we're very, until the last few months, no sweets, very careful about trying to give her organic food, and that kind of thing, and Christy doesn't do that. But it's something I

> can overlook. It's something, where I'm flexible enough on that, that she makes up for it in other ways.

In Cassie Lee's experience, specific childrearing practices did not have to match totally in order for her to feel that there was an adequate level of compatibility. A sense of trust can be built on a process through which mothers and childcare providers resolve differences, not just on sharing the same values. Cassie Lee was aware that the adaptations often go both ways; Christy also changed how she does things in response to Cassie Lee's preferences.

> Christy's bent to our thinking, and some ways we've bent towards hers. She's taught Franny manners, which we'd never done. And, not that I think that's unimportant and that's why I haven't done it, it's sort of one of those things you just never got around to. And because Christy's reinforced saying please and thank you, and stuff like that, we've begun to do that at home. It's sort of a coming-together kind of thing I think with Christy. There's some things that she's emphasized at day care, that we haven't really paid attention to at home, but we've begun to, because she has. I think it's kind of coming, like I said, we bend her way some ways, and she bends to our way, too.

Changing practices allowed greater satisfaction with one's childcare arrangement, both because it aligned practices between the parents and the childcare providers and because it assured mothers that their concerns were being addressed. Having a cooperative relationship with the provider reduced mothers' concerns and fears.

Childrearing partnerships often developed when new parents turned to their providers as experts in child rearing. Early childhood is a period of many changes, for the individual child and for the family. New mothers often seek information about how to handle parenting issues as they arise (Hughes 1985). Mothers saw their childcare providers as important sources of guidance and helpful information. Marie Lowe, a family childcare provider, described how mothers often sought her advice when they brought in or picked up their children. She said:

> Some of them come to me a lot, and say, what should I do about this, and what should I do about that. . . . A lot of times it's "When should I start

> potty training them," "When should I take the bottle away from them." Most of the time they ask me those things, instead of me saying, "Well, don't you think it's time to take the bottle away."

Many of the concerns were immediate, and the childcare provider was often the first person mothers turned to for help. It was easier to ask the childcare provider than to read a book, attend a workshop, or call and visit the pediatrician. The childcare provider knew the particular child and could help mothers figure out an appropriate plan of action to solve their parenting problems. A first-time mother described how much information she got from her childcare providers:

> I always think he has chicken pox, because of blisters, he's getting chicken pox. "No, that's not chicken pox," [they say]. They've kind of guided me along with why is he always pulling at his ear, [they say] "He's got an ear infection." Really? I mean, I didn't know what it was, he had never had one. Take him to the doctor, he's got an ear infection. I mean, I learned little things like that, tidbits of information, that you just, invaluable. Oh, he's going to get diarrhea from that medicine, so, be prepared. He's going to get a bad rash, put baking soda in his bath water. . . . That gets rid of it. Let him run around without his diaper on for an hour. They told me that. You know, I mean, try an antihistamine for that runny nose, he's had it for three weeks. An antihistamine may work. I mean, [they would recommend a] home remedy, that I don't have to take him and spend twenty-five dollars at the doctor's, just to see a doctor, and say, oh [an antihistamine] will work. . . . [The doctors just] end up telling me, half the time, the same thing the daycare told me. I guess [an antihistamine]would help him, oh, okay. . . . I remember when he turned a year old, the lady in daycare said, you know, you can start giving him whole milk now. You can? I called the doctor, oh, if he's a year old, give him whole milk. I didn't know that. I didn't know. That was wonderful.

Gloria Thomas experienced this advice giving as a positive part of her current childcare arrangement:

> I never asked for it at the beginning. I've never . . . they got me into communication. I just, I was a parent that [thought] daycare providers at the beginning were in charge. But this daycare is like, no, you're the parent.

> [They said] We want to help you. How can we help you be a good parent or just be a parent in general? How can we help you with your child? So they're the ones who pulled it out of me. Well come on, now let's get a grip, we have to deal with your child here, what can we do together? So that's why I've been taught a lot with this daycare a lot as far as communicating. Because I guess it's what I always wanted but I never felt comfortable with getting in these other family child cares.

Gloria was willing to learn how to communicate with her childcare providers and appreciated the education and support she was given for parenting, even though she was still often uncomfortable with the social differences between her own African American style and the White middle-class interaction style of the provider.

What is going on here is that mothers were able to use interpersonal relationships to procure services from their childcare providers. Because childcare services were not "one-size-fits-all" or even "buy the right size," the interpersonal relationships allow mothers to navigate inevitable differences with greater ease. Good relations even allowed mothers to ask for modifications in what the childcare providers initially offered as their service.

Childrearing partnerships, more than businesslike and friendship-based childcare arrangements, kept the focus on the child and allowed mothers and childcare providers to negotiate and adapt their childrearing practices to one another. The ability to negotiate and adjust the relationship is what allowed mothers to manage their worries when they had doubts about the quality of care.

Feeling Supported

When these relationships were working well, mothers felt supported by them and worried less about their children. Childcare providers recognized that young parents lacked knowledge, experience, and access to advice about how to parent well. Mrs. Jonas, a family childcare provider for twenty-five years, said:

> I think really, today, the mothering is just hit and miss . . . . I don't think [young parents today] have had very much mothering and they really don't know what to do and how to do it.

One childcare center provider, Keisha Brown, explained how she often lent an ear to mothers:

> Well, I just say, some people . . . might not be close to their families, and they just need somebody to talk to. . . . And, then, sometime it makes them feel better, to have somebody to talk to.

Experienced childcare providers were more confident about giving childrearing advice than new childcare providers, and they also knew when to give it unsolicited and when to wait until parents sought their advice. The usefulness of providers' knowledge and experience to mothers who needed information about child rearing often led to an interdependent relationship between mother and provider.

Most childcare providers were receptive to being asked for their advice on child rearing because they realized that mothers today are under tremendous stress. Mrs. Jonas was acutely aware of how complex and difficult the job of parenting has become in today's society. She said:

> There's so much [more] pressures than there were back forty years ago. Even forty years ago, hey, when I grew up, there was never a lock on our door. We went off on vacation, we never locked anything. What would you do today if you did that? You'd come home you wouldn't find anything; or you'd find somebody living there when you got there. Our times, our morals, our whole system has changed. I don't think it has to do with mothers. I think mothers still love, but I think that when you're earning that bread, you're taking that child, and [wondering, do] you have enough to ends meet and you don't know how things are going to come out and you're getting harassed at work. . . . It's just too much pressure.

The childcare providers I spoke with were quite humble about the important role they played in providing this support and barely acknowledged how much the information and attention that they gave parents supported young families at a critical period in their lives. They extended themselves to young families both because the parents' needs drew them in and because they felt a responsibility for helping young families.

Those working with young children in childcare settings have long recognized the potential for institutions to support young parents and provide parent education. In the late nineteenth and early twentieth centuries, neighborhood-based settlement houses provided childrearing advice along with child care. According to Geraldine Youcha (1995), Jane Addams's Hull House asked mothers to provide daily reports not only on the child's physical state (such as bowel movements) but also on how family time was handled (such as bedtime). In turn, Hull House offered mothers advice on personal hygiene, manners, alternatives to traditional health care practices, clothes making, and cooking. Using childcare arrangements to teach parenting was also a strategy adopted by the early Head Start programs in the 1960s (Wrigley 1987). Following a philosophy of working with the whole family, parents were drawn into participation in their childcare arrangements (a'Beckett 1990). While most of this parent involvement revolves around ways in which parents can support childcare centers, a component of parent involvement includes providing parent education during daily interactions at arrival and departure times (a'Beckett 1990).

The potential for childcare settings to be more than just a place to leave children temporarily is something early childhood educators have long advocated. When parents communicate with their childcare providers, it provides a supportive function for them and their families (Powell 1978a; Powell 1978b). Psychologist Preston Britner has written, "Child care has been compared to an extended family because it often serves as a source of support, especially when parent involvement is common and communication occurs regularly between providers and parent" (1999, n.p.). But Britner rightly goes on to suggest that "child care may be more usefully viewed as a social support, rather than a replacement, for the family." Childcare providers are well positioned to talk about parenting concerns and to provide social support to parents. The daily contact between parents and childcare providers makes childcare providers, almost by default, what have been called "natural helpers," or "professional friends" by the early social workers in the 1920s (Tice 1998, 38 n. 2).

By drawing parents more into the childcare setting and encouraging parental involvement, it is assumed that parents will understand better what is going on and therefore worry less. But most parents of very young children do not have the time to become formally involved in their childcare settings, even though they may want to. When childcare providers reach out to the parents by informally talking to them for a few moments, about either their child or their lives, and give them information, even when not solicited, about how their child's day went, they soothe the parents' worries. Some of the providers I interviewed or heard about from the employed mothers I interviewed did this just by being available to listen and answer questions about daily parenting issues. Others viewed their actions within a larger sociological frame, understanding how family tensions and stresses often are created in response to larger societal pressures, such as the financial necessity of having more than one parent employed, and the isolation of parenting resulting from the increasing lack of community networks and extended families.

In the early 1980s, childcare researchers momentarily revived the idea that childcare providers could provide social support and informal help to families, functioning like extended families or local communities (Bronfenbrenner 1979a; Hughes 1985). These researchers were particularly concerned with children in poor families, but their ideas are easily extendable to working- and middle-class families today who are using paid forms of childcare services in the childcare market. This is an important idea that keeps showing up, then disappearing, in childcare discussions.

Shock Absorbers in the Childcare Market

Caring for children requires a degree of intimacy between the child's family and the childcare provider. In order to provide good care for a young child, providers often needed to know what is going on at home. Since mothers and childcare providers generally saw one another on a daily basis, business arrangements readily become transformed into interpersonal relationships. Mothers and providers conversed not only about the child's well-being but also about general family issues and their own lives as women. The intimate nature of many of the child and family topics that mothers and childcare providers discuss meant that their relationships can become more personalized if both parties allowed them to do so. The dyadic relationship between the child and the provider became a triadic relationship between the child, the provider, and the child's parents. The acknowledgment that childcare arrangements were initially and fundamentally based on business principles did not preclude the possibility that significant personal relationships could emerge within them. Indeed, one of the major findings of this study was how often some mothers and providers established relationships that extended beyond the original business of hiring someone to provide substitute care.

The relationship between mothers and childcare providers was a shock absorber of doubts and worries in the privatized, isolating system of childcare services. The use of paid, market-based child care created new issues for parents, though society has yet to present new models for handling these concerns. Even when child rearing was transformed into a commodified service that mothers purchase, a caring relationship often came to exist between the child's family and the childcare provider.

The uneven quality of childcare services made it difficult for mothers to view childcare providers as simply employees to be hired. Because uncertainty about how to transfer care to others still loomed large, mothers depended heavily on their individual relationships with care providers to feel comfortable about having others care for their children and to find out how well the care was going. The relationship with a childcare provider was a critical component in assessing the quality of care. Defining childcare services as more than contractual labor relationships brought care principles into the work and created interpersonal care-based relationships. The experiences of the mothers I interviewed demonstrate that these relationships can be established even over significant social differences and in market-based childcare services.

Five

Shifting from Individual Worries to Social Advocacy

One of my favorite interview questions was "What have you learned from your childcare providers?" My favorite answer was Marci Washington's: "I've learned how to [be an] advocate for my children." She went on to explain, "I probably learned a little bit more about how to be a little bit more outspoken, because when it's your children, then you have to speak up and say what you want. So, I probably learned that . . . Yeah, just advocating for the child."

Although some mothers hesitated to raise their concerns with their childcare providers, others were quick to do so. Like the mothers who hesitated to ask questions, their actions were motivated by their worries, their confidence fueled by their belief that they were acting in their child's best interests. Mothers who were not so quick to act at first learned how to advocate as they learned how to navigate childcare arrangements and establish relationships with their childcare providers.

Several mothers are exemplary because they were confident about the importance of their roles in shaping the quality of the care their children received. In addition to raising concerns with their childcare providers, they also indirectly advocated for their children by supporting, both within the childcare setting and through political work around childcare issues, the provider's economic and psychological needs. By supporting the working conditions and well-being of the childcare providers and contributing materials to the setting, mothers felt that they helped ensure the quality of care for their children. And by addressing their concerns for their own children, they also improved the quality of care for other children.

Being Advocates for Children

When some mothers did not approve of their childcare provider's practices, they told them straightforwardly. When Marci Washington learned from her daughter that her childcare provider disciplined her son by putting him in the corner, she called her childcare provider right away on a Sunday afternoon. She was so upset and concerned by what she had learned that she felt the matter required immediate attention. It could not wait until Monday. She said:

> I wasn't angry when I was talking to her, and I never had any thoughts about pulling him out. I just was shocked, because I'd never seen him stand in the corner. . . . She said, "Oh, you know, I'm sorry," and . . . so that's the way she manages her kids though, and she didn't think was anything was wrong with that, but she didn't think I would mind.

After expressing her disapproval to her childcare provider, Marci felt the practice would stop and she would not have to worry about it anymore. When mothers felt that their concerns were reasonable, they spoke to their childcare providers or to the directors of the childcare centers. Stephanie Harris said:

> And I don't have any trouble saying what I [am concerned about]. I mean, I'm not a bitchy mom or anything, but if I feel like something's being done wrong, or not done, or over done, then I can find a way to say it, or talk to somebody. It's like "I'm kind of worried about this," or "I'm concerned about this." And usually I've never gotten somebody to tell me like we're not going to do that, or we don't do that; we're not going to talk about that, blah blah blah. They're always like, "Okay, I didn't realize that."

Stephanie was matter-of-fact and forthright about her concerns.

Joyce Lewis explained how she was candid about her concerns in spite of the negative feedback she sometimes received because she recognized that she is supposed to be an advocate for her child:

> If I did anything less I wouldn't be doing my job. And the whole idea of having her there is for her to be some place safe. And I know nobody's going to watch her like I watch her, but I think if they know I watch her that closely, they'll watch her a little bit closer too. And if their motivation is that they don't want to hear my mouth, I don't care. And sometimes I've gotten some, probably a little vibes of displeasure that eventually went away. Because like, well, like one night, I came in to pick her up, and they've got a large room, and . . . the kids were watching TV, and I didn't see an adult immediately. And I called out and nobody answered. So I asked [my daughter] who's around and then I realized that what was going on was a little girl had bitten her lip or something. And so [the childcare providers] were attending to her. The bottom line was two people were looking at [the hurt child] and nobody was looking at the other kids. So I mentioned it to the director and I told her, I'm not trying to get anybody in trouble, and I said while they were attending to her somebody else could've vanished. . . . The director was very nice, very appreciative and told me any time I saw something that concerned me to make sure that I communicated with her about it. So the lady who was in primary charge of them was kind of distant to me for a while after that. . . . But, again, that was one of those things I guess you just have to get over because it was the right thing for me to do for my child and for the others too.

Importantly, Joyce saw this advocacy as good not just for her child but also for all the children in care.

Some mothers not only asked about what concerned them but also instructed their childcare providers how to care for their children. When Sally Trainer realized that her family childcare provider was conducting time-outs differently than how she wanted them to be used, she instructed her childcare provider how to do it differently. She said:

> [My family childcare provider] has a time-out bench that she uses, and I told her that that was fine with me because we have a time-out chair at home. That is our form of discipline. . . . [But] I don't think she had necessarily a real time limit . . . .I don't think that was being used, and I think that I told her that it was important to me, and I think that she now is doing it with most of the kids, [and] that they verbally give back to me

why they were there at the end of the time. I don't think that was happening. And that she tell them in a very even manner why they are being there to begin with.

Mothers who proactively asserted themselves and directly addressed their concerns were motivated by their desire to ensure their children's welfare and to establish clear understanding of how things should be done. They sought out explanations (for example, why is my son standing with his nose in the corner?), as well as asking for changes and special treatment for their individual child (for example, please do time-outs this way) when they were uncomfortable. They expected their concerns to be acknowledged and addressed. When that did not happen, they were unapologetic about terminating unacceptable arrangements. Asking for changes and advocating for their children was a strategy that allowed them to monitor the care and ensure its quality through their childcare provider.

Gaining Confidence to Advocate

It was not easy for mothers to speak up as an immediate response to a concern. Many mothers mulled over whether they should say anything, not only because they doubted the validity of their concerns but also because they were uncomfortable with the interpersonal dynamics of raising their concerns. They were aware that some providers would feel defensive or annoyed. Some mothers were afraid that they would be perceived negatively or that the provider's negative reaction to them would be taken out on their child.

When they moved beyond these fears and decided to speak up, their confidence was bolstered if they had outside justifications for their concerns. Some mothers found strength by drawing on the market principles of the childcare arrangement to justify their requests, believing their positions as the employers or clients of the care service warranted their requests for changes or information. They viewed it as their consumer's right to speak up. Control strategies were utilized when mothers positioned themselves as their childcare providers' employers and articulated their relationship as first and foremost a business arrangement.

Control was also enhanced when the provider worked in the child's home. Although in-home caregivers may not have shared their employers' values and preferences, the location allowed mothers to feel they could control both the environment and the provider's practices. Some mothers prepared all the meals and laid out clothes ahead of time in order to define what their children ate and wore. They often determined what activities children would be involved in during the day and dictated those to the childcare provider. Some mothers did not allow in-home childcare providers to take their children outside of the home. While mothers most often cited safety reasons for this practice, limiting movement was also a way to control the provider. Mothers also defined how childcare providers were supposed to interact with their children. Magdalena Cortez, a Mexican immigrant woman who worked in one child's home, was told by the mother how to read to the child and how to discipline him:

> [One mother said], "Don't tell no to the boy, let him be, let him be free." She was very secure in the way she wanted her son to go. [She would] say never touch the child because [the parents] are in charge to do that, just let us know how come the child does not behave correctly and then we will talk to him.

Magdalena followed these instructions but found it very difficult to do so. She was baffled that the mother thought she could spend so much time with the child without having the means to guide his behavior. She did not challenge the mother's instructions, though, because she assumed that this was what an employee was supposed to do, and she viewed herself as an employee.

Sally Trainer was a mother who asserted herself, making her expectations clear to the family childcare provider to whose home she took her child, but she was not directive like Magdalena's employer. While she was clear about how she wanted things done, she did not give orders. Instead, she raised her ideas in an instructive manner. For example, Sally also asked her family childcare provider, Aurelia, to change her approach to gun play. She said:

> [My child] was coming home playing guns. And there was a boy there who did a lot of that, and I told [my family childcare provider] point-blank, I said, "I don't know if that's something you allow here or not, and I suppose it's your choice, but when a child is playing guns, I would prefer to

> have [my child] given an option of being in another place, not being with that child. And I would like it to be verbalized to her that guns are not okay, guns hurt people. There is no good in guns." And [my family childcare provider] did that, she followed that through.

Sally was not only asking for special arrangements to be made for her child in group care, she was also telling her childcare provider how to handle the situation. Perhaps Sally's confidence came from her previous experience with a childcare center where the childcare providers regularly prompted parents to discuss their concerns with them.

Aurelia also did not feel as if Sally was giving her orders. Rather, Aurelia often agreed with Sally's perspective and altered not only what she did with Sally's child but also her general practices with the children in her care. In this case, Aurelia genuinely welcomed Sally's suggestions because she found them useful in her own efforts to curtail gun play in her home, a problem she had already been trying to resolve. Sally's instructions gave Aurelia a method for realigning her practices with her beliefs. Because Aurelia wanted to improve the quality of care and viewed Sally as an important source of information, the two women often discussed how to handle what was going on. Aurelia said:

> She's really great; I can talk to her about just anything. If one of the kids gets sick or anything, I have any questions, I can just ask or tell her [and she will] find me information and that's really good. . . . It's not that she's going to get all paranoid and really think "Oh my goodness, my kid is . . . " you know . . . And with some of [the parents] you can't do that. You can't let them know before you're sure of something [so instead] if you're not sure don't say anything . . . [With Sally] she, really, you can communicate really good.

Aurelia felt that she and Sally were working as a team to figure out how to provide the best care for all the children. Sometimes that allowed Sally to be the expert; at other times, Aurelia was.

Sally's negotiating style and self-confidence were also supported by her exposure to a formal philosophy about gun play and conflict resolution that she had also learned from a previous childcare arrangement. Shored up by a formal philosophy of care and previous experience, Sally felt confident about educating her family childcare provider on alternative methods of care.

Mothers were also more confident when they were sure about the urgency of their concerns. Urgent concerns called for immediate responses, regardless of the degree of discomfort that mothers might experience. Their children's racial safety was among mothers' highest priorities. After being in a new family childcare home for only a couple of days, Gloria Thomas quickly told a White childcare provider who she perceived as treating Black children less well than White children, "This is not going to work," and she stopped using the childcare arrangement even though she did not have another arrangement lined up. This was a bold act for Gloria, since her low income limited the alternatives available to her.

Mexican American mothers whose children attended predominantly White childcare centers monitored how race and cultural differences were handled and often became involved in efforts to improve cross-cultural interactions. Aurora Garcia informally became the childcare center's multicultural consultant and worked to help the center staff develop better cultural competency. For example, when a White child pretended to be an Indian and came to school stereotypically dressed in feathers and headband, wielding a toy tomahawk and whooping war cries, she intervened. Aurora Garcia told how she corrected for cultural incompetence in this incident:

> There was this one little boy who was totally involved and played Indians and cowboys all of the time and he likes to get painted. . . . I brought it up to them and I told them I was having a little difficult time with the fact that the staff was feeding into this child's fantasy by painting him. That's not how Indian people are. And so when I brought it up, they stopped it, I mean, they realized you're absolutely right.

The childcare center was responsive to her concerns and asked her to work on the problem, so she developed programming to introduce children to multicultural materials and multicultural training for the staff. She also worked with the particular child and his family to make them aware of the problems of stereotypic Indian play.

> But then it was sort of like they asked me to work with them on it, because then it was the other issue of the other parent, and what kind of message that child is getting from the parent. . . . What we did is we bought this book called *The ABCs of the American Indian Way* and it was

> written by an American Indian and so we gave him this book and we talked to him and told him that we're giving you this because we want you to understand Indian people are a lot of different people.

Although Aurora often resented having to work on these issues, they arose often enough to demand continuous attention. Her general concern for a respectful multicultural environment, not just for her child but for all children, motivated her to speak up and help her childcare center develop its multicultural awareness. Having a sense that her acts benefited many, rather than just being an individual child's particular need, gave Aurora confidence to speak up.

By becoming involved in the center's curriculum and working with the staff, Aurora went beyond monitoring the quality of care to create the kind of care that she wanted. When mothers like Aurora and Sally taught their childcare providers how to handle difficult matters, they were both advocating for their children and actively creating a better fit with their childcare providers. These examples suggest that under certain conditions, mothers can influence what happens in the childcare setting.

Mothers also found it easier to speak up about situations in which they could see that a center's own rules or licensing regulations were being violated. When what mothers requested was legitimized by formal rules, it was easier for them to advocate for their children. For example, Gwendolyn Jackson went straight to the director when the staff-to-child ratio seemed wrong:

> Most every day . . . there were just too many children. . . . And, then, when I spoke about it, and mentioned it, they kept promising me that temporary [help] will come, and somebody was going to come, somebody. It was just a matter that the temp hadn't gotten there, or, they always made excuses for why it was uneven, the ratio wasn't correct. But I was the type of mom, I would come all different times of the day, and the ratio would still be off. There would still be no temp, or the person who had cared for the children all day would tell me, "I didn't have any help."

Sometimes mothers drew on the authority of experts to back their concerns, referring to information about such matters as developmentally appropriate childrearing practices or health advice from professionals.

Elizabeth Seymour found it easier to ask her childcare provider to do things differently because she had medical justification for her concern:

> Things that have been hard for me to say to [my childcare provider]. . . . There are little things that I've thought of but [I don't say anything because] I thought, oh, it's probably just me, you can do it that way, it doesn't affect the welfare of children. [But] she did put honey on some bread once and that was one of those things where I had to tell her about honey and babies [that you can't feed honey to babies before they're a year old because of the danger of botulism].

Similarly, when Lupe Gonzalez's aunt took care of her infant daughter, the aunt often relied on the family's traditional childrearing practices and the grandmother's advice, whereas Lupe was guided more by parenting manuals and her pediatrician's advice. Lupe hesitated to tell her aunt what to do, but at the same time she wanted to make sure that her aunt did not do anything wrong. It made it easier when she could state her requests by citing her pediatrician's advice:

> I thought that if I was going to correct her in a way that she would may be get her feelings hurt or something, as in "Don't feed her that food just yet." . . . But [instead of] kind of correcting her and saying, "I don't want her to have that food just yet," . . . I would have to say, "The doctor doesn't want her [to have that yet] . . . she only wants her to have this, this and this," and that was it. At first I thought that maybe [my aunt] would say I am just too overprotective or something, but no, I would kind of point it to the doctor. "The doctor said she can only have this, this and that," and that was that. So it was kind of pointed at saying it was the doctor's idea. And then [my aunt] would accept it.

Depersonalizing the request by attributing it to formal sources such as advice manuals or pediatricians made it easier for mothers to ask for changes, especially from friends or relatives. Lupe also felt that because she paid her aunt to provide care, she was justified in asking her to do things her way, whereas if her grandmother had cared for her baby for free, she would have had to accept whatever care the grandmother wanted to provide.

Viewing themselves as employers, the urgency of demands, a belief in a philosophy of care, a communalistic view of improving conditions for all children, and the ability to rely on experts to back up requests all made it easier for mothers to address their worries in a proactive and productive manner. They felt they had the right and responsibility to act on their child's behalf, and this gave them the confidence to raise their concerns and ask for changes.

Taking Care of Childcare Providers

Mothers were not insensitive to how their requests affected their childcare providers. This awareness not only limited their actions but also motivated them to go beyond formal contractual understandings of the childcare arrangement. In order to mediate possible negative feelings, mothers supported their providers beyond the limited definitions of the business relationship or actual care of the child because they understood that the quality of their children's care was linked to both the financial stability and the psychological well-being of their childcare providers. For example, Denise Johnson noticed that when her family childcare provider was having troubles with her husband, she appeared less joyful around her child and seemed less attentive and less interactive. Personal circumstances affected providers' ability to focus on their work and take good care of the children.

Mothers often extended themselves beyond their own individual childcare needs to try to improve the lives of their childcare workers. They provided numerous forms of informal support to underpaid providers. For example, Bonnie Taylor paid for her Mexican immigrant provider's plane ticket so she could get home regularly to visit her family in Mexico. Schoolteacher Gretchen Hall advised Shari Luchessi about how to address a problem her child was having in school. Julie Lopez provided care for her childcare provider's children during the weekends and evenings, as did Laurie Seitz for Carol Prentice. Andrea Sawyer helped her childcare providers apply for legal permanent residency status. Kathryn Ercolini helped her family childcare provider look for other families who needed care in order to increase her low enrollment.

Lucinda Curtis's home was not only the site for child care, it also provided a gathering place for the several young women who collectively provided care for her son. She described how she made herself available to help them with their personal relationships:

> All three of them will air problems with me. They'll come, and they got a . . . problem, maybe they've got a problem with their relationships. There's another young woman, who used to be a regular, Jan. We don't see much of her anymore. But she's part of the circle of friends. They all know each other, and, one time, Mary and Jan were having problems, and they asked me to mediate what was going on.

Lucinda considered this support an important part of the relationship her family had with the providers, though it extended beyond the realm of child care.

Mothers also made sure that childcare providers understood they were appreciated, even if there was some doubt about the care. While Gwendolyn Jackson asked her providers to change their practices in order to improve the quality of care, she also made sure she let them know what she liked:

> I'm also the type of person, just like I told the director of the first day care, I said, now I complain about things when I see things wrong, I said, but I'm also the type of person, when things are right, I'm going to tell you. And I'm going to show you how much I appreciate that. And, so it wasn't just that I was always complaining. I was helping out. I would stay and help out, whenever I could, or if I had extra time. Particularly in the mornings, sometimes they would be short, but see I would go early enough, before [work], that I could help out a little bit at the beginning.

Gwendolyn's "helping out" meant that she was providing childcare services to other parents when there were staffing shortages.

Joyce Lewis supported her childcare provider indirectly by improving the childcare environment. She was active in efforts to improve the center, both by contributing to events and by donating supplies.

> I think there's balance there, too, because they know that [my husband and I] support them, and I'm sure they know that we have other options for places that we could take our child and we continue to bring her there. And when we get a chance, we do little extra things for the center, like when they had their Memphis in May celebration, after I got my computer, then I printed out some pictures for them to use in decorating the center and made some stickers. So I try to balance it with not just always complaining.

Mothers contributed to the quality of their children's care circuitously by trying to ensure the quality of the childcare providers' work environment and working conditions. Some of this effort was because mothers were genuinely concerned about the provider's well-being—this was the interpersonal dimension of their relationship. Much of it was also motivated by their concern for garnering the best care possible for their child, and achieving that care through giving more than formally contracted for—this was the logic of the business dimension of the arrangement. It was assumed that heightened compensation in the form of support, such as resources, helping in the center, and gifts, might ensure higher quality care. The underlying logic was that a well-treated employee would work harder and do her job better.

Politicization of Mothers' Awareness of Childcare Issues

Mothers also became more involved in supporting their provider and childcare setting when their advocacy for their own children drew them into organized political work around childcare issues. The first step occurred when parents volunteered their time to participate in center governance. For example, Donna Weissman and Jackie Terwilliger served on their childcare centers' parent advisory board and organized fundraisers. They could be counted on as parent volunteers for special events, and because they also knew most of the parents at their centers, they could effectively round up others to help them. They viewed this work as supportive and a demonstration of appreciation for their childcare providers.

Some mothers developed a caring consciousness that made them want to support the childcare site not just for themselves but for other families. For example, Joyce Lewis made use of her higher income and status to contribute to improving the childcare setting for lower-income children. Taking a benevolent perspective on her actions, she described her activities in her center as making a positive contribution to the larger community. She explained:

> Jerome [my husband] and I like to think that we serve a function there too because it's a mix, it's a mixture of professional parents and [the community college] students. So you've got single and divorced, professional people, you've got single moms. So there are things that we can bring

> and expose the other kids to so that everybody gets something out of it. For instance, last year when we had his birthday party at the school . . . they had Winnie the Pooh and he put on like this forty-five minute show. And since Jordan was in open center and everybody's kind of all together, all the kids got to participate. So all the kids got to have a hug from Pooh and they got to dance with him. So it was something that all the kids had fun about and something that a lot of the kids would not really have a chance to do. But, you know, it was a time to celebrate [our son's] birthday, but it was something that the other kids could enjoy too and try. It's kind of giving back as well.

Several mothers of color expressed the conviction that having their children in their racial community was an important component of their child's identity and also reflected the mother's political commitment to their community. Gwendolyn Jackson, an educated, middle-class African American, viewed her presence in a predominantly low-income African American childcare center as a political statement about the importance of knowing one's racial ethnic identity.

> One of the reasons I didn't want to quit the day care I was at, is because, one of the reasons I went is because, the day care was set up for mostly low-income, African American children, and I knew that when I took my child there. That's the first day care. And that's who they were targeting. Well, I felt like, it should be a mixed group of kids, and I felt like my child should know African American children on any level, regardless of class or whatever.

Although she initially enrolled her child in this center simply because she needed care, Gwendolyn quickly found that she had an important role to play in ensuring the quality of care for other children in the center. She could have afforded to leave this center but decided to stay in order to be an advocate for the other children. She believed that her presence helped improve the basic quality of care. She would monitor compliance with licensing regulations, such as adequate staff-to-child ratios. Although she was a critical consumer, she also recognized that the high percentage of low-income parents among center users contributed to some of the problems she saw. The center often failed to be its best because it could not increase its revenue by raising parent fees. Similarly, the parents' hands were tied because they were not in any position to ask for additional services. It seemed to some that they were held hostage to this particular center by their lack of economic options, as well as their lack of knowledge of better care. Gwendolyn said:

> I felt like that if there were some people who [were] of a higher class . . . who . . . would go make them do, [the childcare center] would do. And, therefore all the children would benefit. But if there was a way for [the childcare center] not to do, because they knew that maybe some of these mothers weren't going to be as concerned, or not going to have the time to be on their butt, they weren't going to do.

Gwendolyn felt that it was important for this predominantly African American childcare center to be its best, and she took a politically active position advocating for the other African American parents:

> To look at the day care, it was beautiful, just brand new, but just poorly run. But, I was willing to give it a chance, because it was new and it takes some time to get these things up and running. . . . But I was trying to hold people accountable because this was a beautiful day care. It had beautiful potential. It was right on my way to school, even though I had to go through a little inner-city kind of area. It was fine with me, because they had good security. They had everything. It wasn't like I was putting my child in jeopardy, by her being in that facility. And in the end, I always felt like I was helping the community.

Her efforts were also directed at problems that seemed minor, and easily solved.

> Since they didn't have paper towel, I went and bought paper towel. Since they didn't have certain things for the children, I went and bought it, and I brought it there. That was my way of saying, if you won't take the responsibility, I will. But there weren't very many parents who were going to do that. There weren't very many parents who could afford to do that, and many of the parents who go there were little young girls, trying to finish high school.

Gwendolyn initiated a process of change. Her actions served as an example, and eventually other parents started to address the problems they saw:

> The health department got called, and they swore I had done it. But I actually didn't do it. One of the other parents had taken the initiative. I'm glad. Because I think with seeing me do, it did make them think. It did make them take other initiatives. They didn't feel like they were in it by themselves, and that they could take some of the responsibility.

Gwendolyn believed that she was the catalyst for some of these changes and stayed in a situation that was less than perfect for her own child longer than she might have if she had been looking out only for her child's best interest. She was committed to supporting all the children and the childcare providers at her childcare center by encouraging other parents to expect quality care and trying to empower them to achieve it.

A handful of parents moved from personal concern to broader political consciousness about child care in the United States. Mothers' investments in their local childcare-based community sometimes led them into political advocacy work and identification with a larger community, becoming involved in advocating for improved wages for childcare providers and better meeting the childcare needs of working families. They viewed what was going on in their individual childcare settings as reflecting the lack of concern that the government has for children's well-being. Gwen Kennedy called on the government to take more responsibility for regulating the quality of care. She said:

> I have a lot of fear about privately owned day cares where there wasn't any kind of governmental, no governmental control. . . . There's nobody overseeing it, there's nobody checking in to make sure that things were on the up and up and that the kids were really being taken care of.

Leslie Trumball felt the government could do more to support the childcare system, but she was also cynical about whether the government would actually do anything, stating, "But this is a government that is so stingy. I've been to a lot of other countries, with my friends who are au pairs, that live in those countries, and I don't see the problems in Sweden, England, Denmark, Israel. I don't see the same problems there as I do here, at all." In contrast, Lucinda Curtis thought the government could do a lot more.

> I think that this country really has to reevaluate, I mean, child care extends to the educational thing. We've got a huge problem. We've got these

> kids that are roaming around, drifting anomic, alienated from themselves, because they're in a capitalist system. . . . And, so these kids aren't getting attention, guidance, . . . every other problem we've got, if we want to talk about crime problem, want to talk about education problem . . . you could head this thing up, shore it all up at the front end, by taking care of our youngsters.

In fact, she felt that it would be the humane thing for the government to provide childcare programs that would also have a long-term, positive, preventive effect.

Mothers who had experience with federally funded childcare programs were critical of the existing system and the class disparities within it, especially when government policy did not expect all children to get the same level of care that more well-to-do children received in private child care. Gloria Thomas was disapproving of the lower standards:

> [If it is] the government that's doing it, then it is like you get less; you get only the necessities for the kids. But if it is like a private organization, they get scholarships, or they do this or they do that, they just get more for the kids. Whereas government . . . you're in a bottomless pit, and they don't give you very much, just a place for your kid and that's it.

Between government-subsidized care and expensive, private-pay care is a rung of low-quality, private-pay care settings that also need monitoring.

Many parents, simply by living the experience, developed this political awareness of the need for governmental attention to the childcare problem. Some were drawn into political issues by the childcare center staff, who explicitly raised these issues with parents.

Some parents were invited to attend childcare political rallies, asked to send letters to their elected officials regarding childcare bills, and to participate in Worthy Wages campaigns. Parents willingly found alternative care when centers were closed on Worthy Wage Day. Some parents became involved in improving compensation and appreciation of childcare workers because they realized that working conditions influenced the quality of care that their children received and low wages affected the workers' mental health. Gwen Kennedy said:

> When [my child] was there, they paid their workers well. They gave them paid vacations, paid sick leave and benefits. They knew that by valuing the staff, the staff would stay. They wouldn't have the high-level burnout. They got breaks every day. So I really felt them respecting the staff which was intrinsic in respecting the kids that were there as well. And they did have a very low turnover rate.

They came to understand that childcare providers who are underpaid or lack basic staff coverage are limited in how far they can respond to parents' requests for changes in care practices. Through their efforts to ensure quality care in their individual childcare arrangements, including supporting their childcare providers and improving their working conditions, they came to advocate a larger political agenda as well.

As mothers addressed the quality of care for their own children, they eventually became aware that the whole system of care was hobbled by the lack of public support. For many, advocating for one's child was the first way for them to address their worries, but something else happened. By advocating for their child, they advocated for other children. And by also addressing the needs in the settings and improving conditions for their childcare providers, they became more aware of the larger social system within which this carework was conducted. Their actions led to political awareness of the childcare system, and this moved them beyond understanding their childcare arrangements only as individual choices or simply another private family responsibility. Using this enlarged politicized awareness, mothers became more confident about asking for higher-quality care for their own children.

Conclusion

When Care Works

Do mothers' worries make care work?

Despite the advent of a highly visible childcare market, the responsibility for children in nonparental care remains privatized, and mothers continue to have the executive responsibility for ensuring the quality of that care. Beyond concerns about availability and affordability and enrichment opportunities for their children, mothers are very concerned about the quality of care and the well-being of their childcare providers.

In the context of market-based childcare services, it is easy at first to view the relationship between the mother and the paid childcare provider as a businesslike one, either as employer-employee or client-service provider. Alternatively, parents often use a different language to talk about childcare arrangements and the meaning of the relationships within them. Instead of market terms, they often use familial or school metaphors. The role of the childcare provider is often articulated as "childcare provider as teacher" and "childcare provider as family." Neither of these models fully captures the complexity of what really goes on when a child's care is shifted to a paid childcare provider.

Instead, the practices of mothers and childcare providers construct particularistic understandings as they engage in the process of maintaining childcare arrangements. Each mother develops with her childcare provider a personal understanding of how they are going to define the nature of their relationship and its boundaries, their responsibilities and areas of authority, and how to address differences as they emerge. Most of these paid relationships do not remain within the guidelines and practices of market-based arrangements. Instead, some become very personal, others provide services and support beyond the care of the child, and many transcend the limited notion of childcare provider as childcare worker by challenging the primacy of mothers as solitary child rearer.

The interpersonal relationships mothers established with their child-care providers were critical to how comfortable mothers felt with their childcare arrangements. Their relationship with a provider determined how secure mothers felt about acknowledging and addressing their concerns. Communication with the provider was the primary way that mothers could learn about how their child was doing, which they wanted to know on a daily basis. This means that their childcare arrangements were not just about the relationship between their child and the childcare provider but also extended to a relationship between the mother and the childcare provider. Mothers believed that if the adult relationship was good they had a better chance of ensuring the quality of care their child would get.

I learned that mothers doubt that they can know what is going on every minute in their childcare arrangements, and as a result they worry. Many expressed concerns about the quality of care even though at the same time they reported they were satisfied with their current arrangements and held positive views of childcare experiences as beneficial for their children. They still felt a compelling need to monitor the care closely. When what they observed caused them concern, mothers had to decide how to address their concerns. For families who used paid childcare arrangements, advocating for their infants, toddlers, and preschoolers was an enlarged parenting responsibility that previously was not expected until children entered school.

When mothers felt comfortable interacting with the provider, their sense of trust in the provider's care was stronger. Even in the absence of a sense of social comfort based on social similarity or shared values, mothers who felt they could ask questions and communicate with their childcare provider felt that they were able to monitor and advocate for the quality of their child's care effectively. Yet, ironically, many mothers did not feel confident enough to follow up on their concerns. One source of tension in these relationships was that mothers were not sure how closely they should monitor their childcare arrangements or whether they should try to micro-manage their providers' practices.

The difficulties of communication between mothers and providers are exacerbated by the recent commodification of child rearing and the rising availability of paid childcare services provided by childcare centers, family childcare homes, and paid in-home providers. Paid childcare arrangements bring together two sets of principles—care and market ones—yet, we still lack clearly articulated models for this relationship and clear definitions of the role of childcare providers. Employed mothers find themselves in the middle of a social change with no social template to follow. The model each mother followed was one she created as she used these services. Employed mothers in this study are pioneers in using nonfamily market-based child care. And, as for most pioneers, self-innovation is necessary in order to figure out how to deal with many of the unexpected events and matters that arise. Although the new market of childcare services means that mothers receive support in the form of readily available services, they still do not have the prior experience of using these services or formal guidance in selecting them and maximizing their benefits.

Mothers and childcare providers make care work by bringing the principles of caring into the market-based system. Mothers do this individually by being vigilant about monitoring care. The interpersonal relationships between mothers and childcare providers turn businesslike arrangements into caring relationships, creating an unacknowledged system of care that operates within the formally organized market-based system. The mothers' efforts directly address the situational and emotional needs of all the players in the system: the child, the childcare provider, the mother, and the rest of the family.

On the surface, the larger childcare system is organized around a broad mix of private options—both kin and kith, as well as services that are available to be hired. In the market-based services, the principles of the market and consumerism are the most visible, even though the content of the work is organized around the principles of care. Public discussions about the childcare system articulate the market-based principles more than the care principles. This does not mean that care principles are not important or not in operation. They are. And they are extremely important. However, it is not the formal organization of the system that ensures that these concerns are addressed.

Strategies for Making Care Work within the Childcare System

There are three ways that mothers made care work: how they selected the care, how they monitored the care, and how they worked to change the larger system of childcare services. We need to go beyond the matter of mothers' worries to consider how effective these strategies are for ensuring the quality of care for children.

The selection of care was important because it was a way to enhance mothers' trust and comfort with their childcare arrangements. Yet, in the context of market-based childcare services provided by people who are initially strangers, it is unrealistic to expect a perfect fit. It is not possible to find care that fulfills every criterion of quality that mothers have. For example, given the class and racial structure of the childcare system, it is more difficult to find childcare arrangements that meet parental preferences for both class-based and culturally based definitions of quality. Middle-class Mexican American mothers in Santa Cruz had difficulty finding a good fit because they wanted both to stay within their cultural community by using predominantly Latino childcare settings, but they also wanted the educational opportunities offered by middle-class, predominantly White childcare centers. Because middle-class Latino childcare centers did not exist and the middle-class mothers were ineligible for predominantly Latino childcare centers that served subsidized, low-income families, they could not find what they really wanted. They compromised—most often by accepting Latino family childcare homes when their children were infants and toddlers, then switching them into predominantly White childcare centers with a strong educational curriculum when their children turned three (Uttal 1997). The market does not always provide what parents want.

Because mothers will inevitably encounter practices that cause them concern, matching practices is a short-term strategy, effective only as a screening method during the selection of an arrangement. The other selection strategy—to define child care as offering the child opportunities—is also limited, primarily because it ignores the fact that child rearing goes beyond the social and educational activities children experience as they grow up. When children spend long hours in care, they need more than enrichment opportunities. They need emotional attention and attachment as well as guidance and assistance to navigate their social worlds as they spend time in group care. While enrichment opportunities are important components of the quality of care, other important considerations shape the parents' definitions of the "right" arrangement, including philosophies of child rearing (as distinct from educational curricula), the alignment between the lifestyle and values of the family and the childcare provider, and acknowledgment of the larger ecological context that shapes the child's life (why does the family need child care and why has the family chosen that particular arrangement?). Another way to think about this matter is to ask if being exposed to books, numbers, and other children is enough. Of course the answer is no, which is why mothers conceive of child care more broadly than childhood specialists do. Even when they chose settings that offer the best in terms of material, educational, and social opportunities, they worried about where children were going to get compassionate care if not from the childcare providers.

Selecting a nurturing maternal caregiver is another strategy that only works to reduce the mother's worry about the quality of care if the mother can assure herself that a close, loving relationship between the child and childcare provider actually exists. But because of the fundamental difference between maternal care and nonmaternal child care in terms of a long-term commitment to watch a child go from birth to adulthood, even the best childcare provider is still only at most someone else's mother. Mothers acknowledge that nonmaternal child care probably will neither replace what parents give their children nor be permanent.

To develop real trust, another set of strategies involves what mothers do after they have established an arrangement: they find ways to monitor the care, they develop the confidence to inquire when something seems troubling, and they advocate for children and support their childcare providers. Mothers need to develop trust that the childcare provider knows what she is doing, that she is doing what she says she is doing, and that she will also do what the mother and she agree she should do. Childcare providers also need to have confidence in their own abilities and believe that their experience may sometimes legitimately override the mother's directions. Caregiving involves making autonomous on-the-spot decisions in response to unpredictable situations. A childcare provider who lacks competency and authority to make her own judgments and follows a mother's instructions robotically also makes mothers worry. Especially when child care takes place outside the child's home, mothers need to feel assured that their provider has good judgment and can care for the child in changing conditions. In part this also requires learning to release control of what they cannot control. This relinquishment is only possible, however, if there is trust in the childcare provider's competency to care.

Mothers' concerns are a reasonable outcome of a social system that assumes the primacy of mothers in child rearing yet at the same time allows for many of the activities of child rearing to be commodified and delegated to others. The new context of buying care through market-based services creates the confusing conditions in which mothers make their childcare arrangements. The mothers I interviewed worried about the quality of child care because they feared that if they expressed concern and asked for changes, their arrangements would be jeopardized or providers would take their annoyance out on the children. And they simply were not sure that better alternatives existed, even if they were to change their childcare arrangements.

Until recently, public policy and public opinion have not supported employed mothers, and little attention has been paid to their childcare needs. Yet maternal employment and the use of nonparental childcare arrangements have become common practices, even in the middle class. Now questions are being asked about what kinds of childcare environments are optimal for ensuring the healthy development and well-being of children, how available and costly nonparental childcare arrangements are, whether governments should ensure that working families have access to child care to protect their employment, and how the status and working conditions of childcare providers can be raised to ensure a stable workforce of qualified providers.

This book has added to the list of questions about child care: "How does the relationships between employed mothers and the childcare providers make the childcare system work?" These relationships buffer families against the lack of government regulations to ensure quality, protect them from economic practices that make childcare arrangements unstable (such as low-paid workers, nonprofitability of childcare services, and high costs of child care), and cope with gender ideologies that privatize the responsibility of child rearing. This is as much a practical question as an academic one.

How would the formally organized system need to change in order to reflect the concerns expressed in this book and mothers' unacknowledged efforts to make care work? It would need to recognize that the most important elements of the system are the human relationships, between the childcare provider and the child as well as between the adult family members and providers. The organization of care work would support these. By providing time—which only comes through lower staff-to-child ratios, or more adults per setting—this quality of care would be achieved. Training in communication and helping parents learn that they have the right and responsibility to raise their concerns would also heighten the centrality of care principles. Taking the time to talk about the child's care would ensure the quality of care. Communication, however, does not have to take place directly between the parent and the childcare provider. Parents need ways to think about their concerns, help with deciding whether to address their concerns, and guidance in how to address their concerns, even before they speak directly to the childcare provider. The quality of caring also improves when the staff is educated in thinking about the child as holistically located in a family and how to support both the child and the child's parents.

When we listen to mothers talk about their childcare experiences, we learn about the centrality of the childcare provider and about mothers' ongoing efforts to monitor the quality of care from afar. I propose expanding the definition of quality of care to go beyond the physical and material conditions of care, beyond the social and educational opportunities given to the individual child, and even beyond the focus on just the relationship between the childcare provider and the child. The transfer of a child's care from parents to others also involves the adult relationships that surround and manage that care. This new definition has implications for research, practice, and policy, which are laid out in the following sections.

Research Implications

Most childcare studies focus either on the child's well-being and the outcomes of time spent in nonparental care or on the availability and affordability of services to the family. When mothers are studied, they are asked about their satisfaction levels, preferences and criteria for choosing care, and frequency and content of parent-provider communications. By measuring these static variables, we fail to study the social process that constructs this social experience. This is not a complete or fully articulated way of thinking about what the experience of using childcare arrangements means to mothers.

Given what this study tells us about mothers' lived experience, we need to expand how we understand child care. Nonparental care is being asked to provide more than a safe place for children to be parked temporarily during their parents' absence. Further, parental child rearing is also being transformed by the increased use of nonparental care.

Develop a Language That Articulates the Different Kinds of Childcare Philosophies and Shared Childrearing Models

First, researchers need to identify concepts that would give mothers the language to articulate the kinds of childcare arrangements they want. I found that mothers were more confident with questioning and directing the care of their children when they were more able to articulate their own philosophy of care or use the knowledge of experts to justify their expectations. For example, Sally Trainer worked very proactively with her childcare provider about how to do time-outs and to think about gun play, and Elizabeth Seymour and Lupe Gonzalez asked their caregivers not to feed their infants honey. Having concepts or ideas guided mothers' articulation of what they wanted.

I also learned from the mothers in this study that values are central to their experiences, although sharing values was not the primary determinant of successful relationships. Many mothers demonstrated how they worked across differences—racial, ethnic, and economic, as well as differences in childrearing practices—to achieve working relationships and develop childrearing partnerships. A language that better articulates some of their implicit childrearing philosophies would better capture the range of values held about child rearing. In addition to the philosophy of social, emotional, and cognitive development, developing a vocabulary that identifies different cultural notions of child rearing, such as ethnotheories of child development, would be useful.

Conduct More Studies of How Childrearing Is Being Shared

Researchers could better describe what the social practices really look like. To do so they need to examine new models of shared child rearing, determine how families shift child rearing to nonfamilial caregivers, and ascertain how this shapes expectations of paid child care that are different from past ones. Instead of narrowly focusing on how mothers fulfill their mothering functions despite their outside employment, the research question would be shifted to understanding how child rearing is being shared by multiple adults. Researchers would ask parents to identify which components of child rearing are shared with childcare providers, how they share child rearing with their childcare providers, and how they negotiate differences in childrearing practices. For example, the researcher might ask in an in-depth interview, "What elements of child rearing do you think can be transferred to childcare providers?" and "When you don't agree on child rearing, how do you and your childcare provider resolve these differences?"

Include Fathers in Studies

Research on paid childcare arrangements needs to expand to include fathers' views of paid childcare arrangements and ask them how they participate in the management and responsibilities of these arrangements. One of the dilemmas of using nonparental childcare arrangements is the overwhelming sense of responsibility for constantly monitoring the quality of that care. Several of the mothers mentioned fathers' involvement in carrying out activities related to child care, although almost all the mothers maintained that they had the executive responsibility of managing and monitoring care. In order to understand accurately the role of fathers, mothers need to be asked about why they feel this responsibility is theirs, but fathers also should be asked directly about their understandings and experiences with childcare arrangements. Do they feel that they are excluded and pushed away from greater involvement? Are they aware of how much mothers are thinking about the care? Or is their involvement partial because they are not aware of the broad range of responsibilities involved in delegating the care of one's child to other people?

Explore How Different Types of Care Matter

This analysis has not paid much attention to how different types of market-based care shape relationship dynamics, and it begs the question whether different types of care—large group care by credentialed staff or small group care by nonprofessionals—make a difference. My first response is that given the isolation of parents in navigating their individual arrangements and the variety of childcare providers found in different settings, the type of care is not as urgent a condition as who the childcare provider is. A self-employed family childcare provider may be just as stressed out as a center worker, but for different reasons. A provider in any of these settings could encourage communication and be able to develop a more intimate relationship with a child and family. However, I think it would be foolish to ignore how the working conditions influence the psychological availability and well-being of the worker. These may not be strictly tied to the type of care, but to the labor relations in the setting. The relationship between labor conditions and the quality of care needs further exploration by researchers.

Analyze How Race and Class Differences between Families and Childcare Providers Structure These Relationships

From the numerous examples provided by this study, it is clear that race and class structure childcare experiences. I have not, however, fully examined how they impact upon the relationships, except to mention that different types of childcare services are given to children of different social classes and that mothers are aware of race and ethnic differences, as well as race and class stratification, that influence their childcare options. (See also Julia Wrigley's work on this topic.) There could be more of how race and class status shape the dynamics between mothers and childcare providers, especially in terms of how value differences are negotiated. (See the work being done by sociologists such as Mary Tuominen, Cameron Macdonald, and Julia Wrigley, who examine the labor relationship between women of different social classes and race and ethnic groups.) One of the major findings of this study is that women of color—especially African American women—view child care as not just an individual choice but as one that they exercise as members of a racial ethnic community. The racialization of Latinas as "natural nurterers" was also briefly touched upon, but what this objectification means in terms of a larger labor force and the availability and recruitment of workers, especially immigrant women, and the impact on the quality of care, also needs to be analyzed.

Practical Implications

The new understandings of nonparental childcare arrangement identified here also have implications for practice and policymaking. The childcare system provides parents with a wide variety of options, yet parents, especially those who are first-time users of childcare services, appear to be exposed to only one or two of these options. This creates a kind of tunnel vision about the full range of possibilities. Because of the newness of the experience, both as a system that has emerged within contemporary society and the uniqueness of experience within the lives of individual parents, this book ends with proposals for how public support for nonparental childcare arrangements could be made available, particularly in ways that would not remove from families the responsibility for their individual children, but would help parents with the responsibility of ensuring quality care. The uniqueness of their individual experiences makes it hard to lay out clear guidelines for how parents should proceed or what should be done to support them. These proposals recognize the heterogeneity of the organization of nonparental childcare arrangements as well as the distinctiveness of the individual families that use them.

Inform Parents of the Full Range of Criteria They Can Use to Select Childcare Arrangements

New parents lack the parenting experience to evaluate the quality of caregiving. The scarcity and cost of different types of care (such as infant care) further compound the difficulty of the search. The initial selection of a childcare arrangement is a complex one because there are many factors to consider: child-centered factors and adult-centered factors, different types of child care (e.g., center-based, family childcare homes, nannies and other paid in-home childcare providers), as well as the philosophy that shapes childcare practices in a particular setting. Both the environment and interpersonal relations—for the child and the parent—need to be evaluated. Additional questions that could be added to the standard checklist given to parents to evaluate a childcare choice include:

1. What is the childcare provider's philosophy about child rearing?
2. How does the childcare provider want to communicate with parents?

3. How does the childcare provider want the parent to communicate their concerns?
4. What method will parents and childcare providers use to discuss differences in childrearing practices?

The criteria should cover how childcare arrangements include and affect adults as well as children. Parents seeking care are not routinely advised to select their child care holistically on the basis of what it will mean to them, not just their children. Parent-oriented advice usually stops short at considerations of convenience, cost, and availability, but some employed mothers are more comfortable with their child care than other mothers are because their evaluation also took into account the kind of relationship they wanted to have with their childcare provider. Parents should be advised that their sense of fit, not only between the child and the childcare provider but also between themselves and the childcare provider is an important consideration in the selection process.

Teach Parents to be Advocates

Parents would benefit from learning to be advocates for their children, especially given the absence of uniform standards and high quality controls from the government. When parents, especially new ones, first engage childcare services, they are often unaware of the mix of market and care principles. Once in an arrangement, they begin with assumptions that are shaped first by market principles. Educating parents about the mix of market and care principles would inform them of their responsibility to monitor the care. A formal understanding that it is their role to advocate for the child may enable them to act more confidently in the midst of mixed principles and competing messages.

It is vital to provide support for parents to address their concerns and negotiate their childcare arrangements, even after they have established them. Since the discovery of differences is inevitable, providing parents with methods to discuss differences is necessary. Developing an understanding that differences are to be expected and that negotiating differences is learned in practice could help parents navigate the process. When misunderstandings arise, parents need ways to address their concerns. Sometimes the first step is not direct confrontation with the childcare provider but being able to think out loud about one's concerns. They also need to know that changing practices rather than terminating arrangements is a possible solution. Possible strategies include:

- Identifying a primary childcare provider for each child so the parents know who their "point person" is.
- Providing a childcare crisis hotline for parents to voice their doubts.
- Providing a process for communicating concerns.
- Establishing mediation services that help parents and childcare providers discuss their differences.
- Providing parent guides that explain how parents can discuss their concerns.

One example of this type of guide was written by Janet Gonzalez-Mena (2000) for childcare providers. In it, she describes the RERUN method, a process by which childcare providers can recognize and address differences. She points out that sometimes the resolution to differences is not doing either what the parent wants or what the provider wants but finding a third way that respects both the parent's and provider's ways of doing things. RERUN stands for ***reflect*** the feelings of others and self-reflect; ***explain*** your perspective after listening; give ***reasons*** for one's explanations; ***understand*** yourself and the other person's perspective; and ***negotiate*** your understandings of one another. The goal is to share reasons and power, and to reach a mutually acceptable outcome. A similar guide is needed from the parents' perspective.

Recognize the Care Providers' Expertise and Role in Childrearing When the Care of a Child Is Shared by Multiple Adults

Childcare providers develop highly intimate understandings and in-depth knowledge about the particular children with whom they regularly spend many hours. When mothers need more support for parenting, they often turn for advice to their childcare providers rather than their partners, extended families, or neighbors. This is not surprising, since the users of childcare arrangements are often new parents who are in the process of learning how to care for a young child and their child care arrangement gives them the opportunity to regularly interact with the people who are caring for their children. Childcare providers sometimes have years of experience caring for young children and, based on their experiences, can give ideas and advice to parents. Thus, childcare arrangements have the potential to provide social support and parenting education, although this needs to be more explicitly acknowledged as an important component of the service offered by childcare providers to parents. It would be beneficial to provide training for childcare providers to expand their expertise in parent education as well as child development so that they can act as parenting consultants and support persons. In-service training provided by childcare centers or family childcare associations could accomplish these goals. More attention needs to be focused on training childcare providers to be active participants in this relationship, both in terms of initiating dialogue with parents and responding nondefensively when parents raise concerns.

Develop a System of Titles for Childcare Providers

Childcare providers who can articulate their philosophies of child rearing, especially in group care, will provide parents with a better understanding of what guides their practices. For example, when childcare providers tell parents that they view themselves as "educarers," as suggested by Magda Gerber's philosophy of adult-infant interaction (Gerber 2001), they indicate to parents how they mix caregiving and educational opportunities. A provider who wants parents to work as a team with her could articulate her role as "co-parent" or "co-childrearer." Alternatively, the provider who views herself first and foremost as an educator could present herself as a "preschool teacher." The development of a system of titles would reveal the hidden philosophies of care that already informally exists in practice.

Organize Care around Family Support Rather than Individual Development

Since children are the direct recipients of childcare services, the services formally offered are often narrowly defined in terms of the child's needs (such as quality of physical environment and child-provider relationship, educational opportunities, staff-to-child ratios). It would change the way care is organized and evaluated if we moved to an organization of nonparental childcare as offering services that function to support the entire family, including the working parents and siblings who may not be directly in care.

Childcare centers and family childcare providers could provide information newsletters, a resource center or reading room, parenting workshops, and parenting support groups. It would also be helpful to organize the times when parents leave and pick up their children to encourage interactions, including requiring parents to make contact with their primary childcare provider.

A structural change that would enable better communication and parent education would be to lengthen the workday of childcare workers to thirty minutes after the last child has gone home. This would allow childcare providers to focus on parents and children at pickup, rather than having their attention divided by trying to clean up at the same time.

Who Can Ensure a Broader Understanding of Quality of Care?

I hope this book shows how central the mother-provider relationship is to the quality and practices that ensure children's well-being in nonparental care arrangements. The care of young children is deeply embedded in adult relationships and in social, economic, and political structures. This dimension of child care is often ignored in research, practice, and policy. By revealing the actual practices, I hope this will change. Discussions of the quality of nonparental care focus narrowly on the curricular content and neglect a full examination of the range of the child's needs in care, including the adult relationships that oversee it. Now more than ever we must turn our eyes toward this relationship because there are limits to how much the invisible work that employed mothers and childcare providers do together can effectively ensure the stability and quality of children's care. The privatization of the responsibility for child rearing is ideologically narrow and increasingly dysfunctional in practice.

In the past, the privatization of child rearing within networks of relatives and neighborhoods meant that government could take a hands-off stance toward child rearing and the childcare needs of working families. But, today, as these traditional, community-based sources of care become less readily available, the interpersonal relationships between two groups of women—employed mothers and paid childcare providers—must work hard to fulfill the functions that traditional neighborhoods and extended families used to provide. Together, mothers and childcare providers ensure the quality of care that a child needs to grow up into a healthy adult. Without greater public and spousal supports, employed mothers turn to childcare providers, the only other adults who regularly share the daily issues of hands-on child rearing with the mothers. The voices of worry that are expressed in this book capture interpersonal relationships that are struggling to make a system of contradictory principles and messages work. Mothers and childcare providers are using their partnership to provide caring relationships within the ill-fitting contours of market transactions. The significance of the relationship between employed mothers and childcare providers is heightened by its isolation—from public policy, from public issues, from public support, and even from other family members.

Even the best individual childcare provider cannot overcome the deficits of a low-quality physical environment, understaffing, the lack of training of childcare providers, or the demoralization caused by the low status of the work. The recognition of child care as a family support service instead of a holding place for children justifies spending more resources on improving the quality of the care. When we recognize that parents are sharing care and communicating with their childcare providers in the best interests of the child, then we can shape policies that best support positive forms of this relationship. The quality of childcare services also needs to be improved through better and higher standards of licensing and regulation of all childcare settings.

Obviously, child care based on a richer definition and higher standards of quality would be desirable, but the real question is, who is responsible for ensuring this quality? Government regulation, support, and intervention have been resisted as undermining the authority of private families. Women, who have historically done this work unrecognized and for the most part without pay, now object to the assumption that this work automatically should be done by them, especially without any support from other sources. Childcare providers absorb the costs of care by working for far less than the real social value of their work. Women want quality child care, but if they temporarily withdraw their free or underpaid childrearing services in order to encourage attention by policymakers and the participation of men, they endanger the well-being of children. Most mothers and childcare providers are not willing to take this risk.

As a system, childcare arrangements are unstable, and if it were not for the extraordinary efforts of mothers and childcare providers to sustain them, they would probably be even more fragile. The individual efforts of mothers and childcare providers, in spite of the lack of societal support, ensure that differing values and differences do not lead to the breakdown of childcare arrangements and that arrangements have some stability.

Finally, what is the answer to the satisfaction puzzle? Why do satisfaction surveys repeatedly find high levels of satisfaction, even though when mothers talk about child care they express so many worries and concerns? One possible answer is that mothers avoid acknowledging problems in their childcare arrangement because that would require change, or else expose them to the risk of being viewed as neglectful mothers. Ultimately, however, I came to understand it differently. Mothers were not in denial when they simultaneously reported high levels of satisfaction and worries in their interviews. Worrying was the process by which they could develop confidence in their childcare arrangements. Their worrying was evidence that they were monitoring their childcare arrangements and making efforts to ensure the quality of the care. Worrying was a response to the contradiction of having responsibility for monitoring their children's care, even when they could not know what was going on in care. Doubts did not become endless worries, but instead were catalysts for positive attention to the quality of childcare arrangements and motivated action. Although they had doubts and concerns, many mothers were able to establish trusting relationships with their childcare providers because the mothers put effort into making care work.

Making care work means worrying—worrying about the quality of care for the child, about the well-being and working conditions of the childcare provider, and about the government that should be doing more. Care works when mothers are able to talk to their childcare providers about their inevitable concerns. When care works, mothers can responsibly leave their children with others, knowing that their children are being well cared for.

Appendix
Respondents in Order Interviewed

Pseudonym	Current primary childcare arrangement	Number of hours worked per week	Primary job	Occupation status	Family income	Her annual income
Santa Cruz Interviews 1990–1993						
Sally Trainer	Family childcare home	35	Physician assistant	Lower middle	$12,250	$12,250
Becky Muller	Childcare center	20	Housing coordinator	Lower middle	$37,500	$12,000
Gretchen Hall	Family childcare home	24	Schoolteacher	Upper middle	$76,550	$42,550
Linda Molina	In-home care provider	40	Assembly worker	Entry level	Unknown	$12,000
Jana Swift	Family childcare home	46	Assistant manager	Upper middle	Unknown	Medium
Nancy Lopata	Family childcare home	40	Receptionist	Lower middle	$20,880	$20,880
Elena Romero	Childcare center	25	Nutritionist	Upper middle	High	$14,118
Laurie Seitz	Family childcare home	40	Rec. program coordinator	Upper middle	High	$28,000
Lois Polanski	In-home care provider	40	College professor	Professional/ Executive	$35,000	$35,000
Denise Johnson	Family childcare home	40	Warehouse supervisor	Lower middle	$60,000	$30,000
Sylvia Rodriguez	In-home care provider	42	Office manager	Upper middle	$41,292	$24,192
Aurora Garcia	Childcare center	40	City administrator	Upper middle	$84,000	$40,000
Lupe Gonzalez	Family childcare home	40	Administrative assistant	Lower middle	$41,558	$22,838
Elaine Ghio	Childcare center	40	Clerical worker	Upper middle	$34,908	$28,536
Kathryn Ercolini	Family childcare Home	45	City administrator	Professional/ Executive	$63,352	$39,400
Lisa Garni	In-home care provider	40	Lawyer	Professional/ Executive	$50,000	$50,000
Elizabeth Seymour	In-home care provider	>20	Self-employed home business	Lower middle	Unknown	$12,000
Wendy Thompson	Childcare center	36	Sales manager	Lower middle	$52,000	$28,000
Julie Lopez	Childcare center	37.5	Outreach specialist	Lower middle	$22,238	$22,238

Race/ ethnicity	Marital status	Number of children	Age of preschool children (year)	Mother's age	Mother's years of school	Class status (see note)
Santa Cruz Interviews 1990–1993						
White	Single parent	1	4	34	13.5	Stable low income
White	First marriage	1	4	28	16	Middle
White	First marriage	2	0.5	31	18	Middle
Mexican American	Living with partner	2	1	31	14	Stable low income
White	First marriage	2	3, 4	32	16	Middle
Guamanian American	Single parent	1	4	24	14	Stable low income
Mexican American	First marriage	3	3, 4	37	16	Upper
White	First marriage	2	0.75, 3	33	19	Middle
African American	Divorced	2	0.5	41	19	Middle
White	First marriage	2	<1	33	13	Middle
Mexican American	First marriage	2	3	28	18	Middle
Mexican American	Living with partner	1	4	39	18	Upper
Mexican American	First marriage	1	0.9	23	12	Stable low income
White	Divorced	1	4	31	13	Stable low income
White	Second marriage	1	3	42	23	Middle
White	Single parent	1	3	37	17	Middle
White	First marriage	2	0.5, 3.0	27	15	Middle
White	Living with partner	2	3	39	16	Middle
African American	Divorced	2	5	32	14	Stable low income

Pseudonym	Current primary childcare arrangement	Number of hours worked per week	Primary job	Occupation status	Family income	Her annual income
Maria Hernandez	Family childcare home	28	Office worker	Entry level	$33,400	$12,600
Gloria Thomas	Childcare center	24	Waitress	Entry level	Unknown	Low
Cathy Perry	Childcare center	42.5	Taxi company dispatcher	Entry level	$40,778	$26,378
Andrea Sawyer	In-home care provider	40	Sales manager	Upper middle	$59,856	$23,856
Deidre Lewis	Childcare center	24	Administrative assistant	Upper middle	$62,636	$27,636
Diane Gomez	Family childcare home	40	Administrative assistant	Lower middle	Unknown	$13,440
Frances Trudeau	Childcare center	65	Lawyer	Professional/ Executive	$68,000	$50,000
Mary Turner	Childcare center	>2.5	Gardener	Lower middle	$67,500	Low
Gwen Kennedy	Childcare center	40	Assistant director	Upper middle	$46,008	$23,208
Bonnie Taylor	In-home care provide	65	Vice-President small company	Upper middle	Unknown	$45,000
Memphis Interviews 1996–1997						
Lisa Barnes	Childcare center	45	Lab technician	Lower middle	$54,070	$20,070
Darcy Reinhardt	Childcare center	40	Vice-President large company	Professional/ Executive	High	High
Stephanie Harris	Childcare center	35	Administrative assistant	Lower middle	$25,200	$25,200
Patty Dawson	Family childcare home	40	Administrative assistant	Lower middle	$32,640	$16,000
Donna Weissman	Childcare center	25	Director, non-profit agency	Professional/ Executive	High	$18,500
Lucinda Curtis	In-home care provider	45	Self-employed consultant	Professional/ Executive	$65,000	$40,000
Gwendolyn Jackson	Childcare center	30	Doctor	Pofessional/ Executive	Medium	Medium
Karen Weiss	Childcare center	>30	Legal secretary	Lower middle	Unknown	Medium
Jane Gilligan	Childcare center	40	Sales manager	Upper middle	$73,000	$33,000

Race/ ethnicity	Marital status	Number of children	Age of preschool children (year)	Mother's age	Mother's years of school	Class status (see note)
Mexican American	Living with partner	1	4	31	16	Stable low income
African American	Divorced	2	5	30	12	Stable low Income
White	First marriage	3	0.8, 3	28	13	Middle
White	First marriage	3	1	30	12	Middle
African American	First marriage	3	0.8, 4	36	16	Middle
Mexican American	Living with partner	3	4	33	10	Stable low income
African American	Living with partner	2	5	35	23	Upper
White	First marriage	2	<1, 3-5	30	18	Upper
White	Living with partner	1	4	38	19	Middle
African American	First marriage	2	<1	28	17	Middle
Memphis	**Interviews 1996–1997**					
White	Second marriage	3	2, 4	30	18	Middle
White	Second marriage	2	4	40	20	Upper
African American	Divorced	2	3	37	13	Stable low income
White	First marriage	1	1.25	22	13	Stable low income
White	First marriage	3	0.8, 3	38	19	Upper
White	First marriage	1	2	32	23	Middle
African American	First marriage	1	0.8	35	23	Middle
White	Married	2	3, 5	Unknown	Unknown	Middle
White	First marriage	2	0.5, 3	37	23	Upper

Pseudonym	Current primary childcare arrangement	Number of hours worked per week	Primary job	Occupation status	Family income	Her annual income
Brenda Sharpe	Childcare center	60	Accountant	Upper middle	$90,000	$50,000
Lashawna Bostic	Childcare center	35	Data entry operator	Entry level	$24,400	$24,400
Francine Wellington	In-home care provider	45	Accountant	Professional/ Executive	$60,000	$60,000
Melissa Berger	Childcare center	30	Sales assistant	Upper middle	$63,000	$28,000
Jackie Terwilliger	Childcare center	>30	President, small business	Professional/ Executive	High	High
Marci Washington	Family childcare home	>30	Nurse	Upper middle	Medium	Low
Cassie Lee Smith	Family childcare home	36	Restaurant owner	Upper middle	$50,000	$20,000
Vanessa Grey	Childcare center	44	Vice-President small company	Upper middle	$23,750	$23,750
Joyce Lewis	Childcare center	40	Social worker	Upper middle	$82,994	$42,994
Leslie Trumball	Childcare center	27.5	Sales clerk	Entry level	$25,500	$13,500

Note on Class Categorization

Composite subjective assessment based on family income, occupational status, marital status, additional income sources, status and stability of jobs, education, apparent material wealth (house, clothes, household furnishings, cars, activities, etc.), ideas expressed in interviews

Upper class: Combined family or single income is high, professional occupation(s), highly educated or have high-status jobs, material wealth obvious, lifestyle and choices enhanced by income.

Middle class: Combined family or single income is solid, managerial but not necessarily professional occupations, having undergraduate education but not professional or higher education degrees, material wealth appears very good, lifestyle and choices only mildly circumscribed by income.

Race/ ethnicity	Marital status	Number of children	Age of preschool children (year)	Mother's age	Mother's years of school	Class status (see note)
White	Second marriage	1	1.5	31	16	Upper
African American	Single parent	1	5	24	14	Stable low income
White	Divorced	1	1	37	23	Middle
White	First marriage	1	0.9	24	16	Middle
African American	First marriage	3	2, 4	Unknown	Unknown	Upper
African American	First marriage	2	2, 5	Unknown	Unknown	Middle
White	Married	1	1.5	31	16	Middle
African American	Divorced	1	4	27	15	Stable low income
African American	First marriage	1	4	42	18	Middle
White	Living with partner	2	3	24	14	Stable low income

Stable low income class: Combined family or single income stable but low, occupational status may be entry level or lower middle, may not have college education, income constricts choices, less money appears to be spent on material things, choices are definitely circumscribed by income.

References

a'Beckett, C. 1990. "Parent/Staff Relationships." In *Trusting Toddlers: Planning for One to Three-Year-Olds in Child Care Centers*, edited by A. Stonehouse. 128–141. St. Paul, Minn.: Toys 'n Things Press.

Apple, R. D. 1997. "Constructing Mothers: Scientific Motherhood in the Nineteenth and Twentieth Centuries." In *Mothers & Motherhood: Readings in American History*, edited by R. D. Apple and J. Golden. 90–110. Columbus: Ohio State University Press.

Belsky, J., and M. J. Rovine. 1988. "Nonmaternal Care in the First Year of Life and the Security of Infant Parent Attachment." *Child Development*. 59, no. 1:157–167.

Bird, C. 1997. "Gender Differences in the Social and Economic Burdens of Parenting and Psychological Distress." *Journal of Marriage and the Family*. 59 (November): 809–823.

Blackwell, M.S. 1997. "The Republican Vision of Mary Palmer Tyler." In *Mothers & Motherhood: Readings in American History*, edited by R. D. Apple and J. Golden. 31–51. Columbus: Ohio State University Press.

Bowlby, J. 1951. *Maternal Care and Mental Health*. 2nd ed. World Health Organization, Monograph Series no. 2. Geneva: World Health Organization.

Breckenridge, S., and E. Abbott. 1917. *The Delinquent Child and the Home: A Study of the Delinquent Wards of the Juvenile Court of Chicago*. New York: Russell Sage Foundation.

Britner, P. A. 1999. "What Leads to Satisfaction for Child Care Providers and Parents?" <http://www.nncc.org/Research/satisfaction.html>.

Bromer, J. 1999. "Cultural Variations in Child Care: Values and Actions." *Young Children*. 54:72–78.

Bronfenbrenner, U. 1979a. "Contexts of Childrearing: Problems and Prospects." *American Psychologist*. 34:844–850.

———. 1979b. *The Ecology of Human Development: Experiments by Nature and Design*. Cambridge, Mass.: Harvard University Press.

Bryant, D., R. M. Clifford, D. Cryer, M. Culkin, S. Helburn, C. Howes, S. Kagan, and E. S. Peisner-Feinbert. 1995. "Cost, Quality and Outcomes of Child Care Centers." University of Colorado at Denver, University of Colorado at Los Angles, University of North Carolina, and Yale University. <http://www.fpg.unc.edu/~NCEDL/PAGES/cq.htm>.

Camasso, M. J., and S. E. Roche. 1991. "The Willingness to Change to Formalized Child Care Arrangements: Parental Considerations of Cost and Quality." *Journal of Marriage and the Family*. 53 (November): 1071–1082.

Capizzano, J., G. Adams, and F. Sonenstein. 2000. "Child Care Arrangements for Children under Five: Variation across States." *The Urban Institute*. Series B, no. B–7, March.

Casper, Lynn. 1995. "What Does It Cost to Mind Our Preschoolerers?" *U.S. Bureau of the Census, Current Population Reports*. P–70, no. 52, Washington, D.C. <http://blue.census.gov/prod/1/pop/p70–52.pdf>.

———. 1996. "Who's Minding Our Preschoolerers?" *U.S. Bureau of the Census, Current Population Reports*. P–70, no. 53, Washington, D.C. <http://www.census.gov/prod/www/abs/msp70–53.html>.

Chang, G. 1994. "Undocumented Latinas: The New 'Employable Mothers.'" In *Mothering: Ideology, Experience and Agency,* edited by E. Nakano Glenn, G. Chang, and L. R. Forcey. 259–286. New York: Routledge.

"The Child-care Dilemma." *Time*. June 22, 1987, 54–60, 62.

Clarke-Stewart, A. 1993 (1982). *Daycare*. Rev. ed. Cambridge, Mass.: Harvard University Press.

Colen, S. 1989. "'Just a Little Respect': West Indian Domestic Workers in New York City." In *Muchachas No More*, edited by E. M. Chaney and M. Castro.171–194. Philadelphia: Temple University Press.

Coontz, S. 1992. *The Way We Never Were*. New York: Basic Books.

Daly, A. 1982. *Inventing Motherhood: The Consequences of an Ideal*. New York: Schocken Books.

Davies, M. W. 1994. "Who's Minding the Baby? Reproductive Work, Productive Work, and Family Policy in the United States." In *More Than Kissing Babies? Current Child and Family Policy in the United States*, edited by F. H. Jacobs and M. W. Davies. 27–64. Westport, Conn.: Auburn House.

Ehrensaft, D. 1987. *Parenting Together*. New York: Free Press.

Endsley, R. C., and P. A. Minish. 1991. "Parent-Staff Communication in Day Care Centers During Morning and Afternoon Transitions." *Early Childhood Research Quarterly*. 6:119–135.

Essig, M., and D. H. Morgan. 1946. "Adjustment of Adolescent Daughters of Employed Mothers to Family Life." *Journal of Educational Psychology*. 37:228–229.

Fagan, J. 1994. "Mother and Father Involvement in Day Care Centers Serving Infants and Young Toddlers." *Early Child Development and Care*. 103:95–101.

———. 1997. "Patterns of Mother and Father Involvement in Day Care." *Child & Youth Care Forum*. 26, no. 2:13–126.

Fenichel, E., A. Griffin, and E. Lurie-Hurvitz. 1998. "Quality Care for Infants and Toddlers." Report prepared by ZERO TO THREE: National Center for Infants, Toddlers and Families for Child Care Bureau Administration on Children, Youth and Families, Administration for Children and Families, Department of Health and Human Services <http://nccic.org/pubs/qcare-it/quest.html>

Fisher, B., and J. Tronto. 1990. "Toward a Feminist Theory of Caring." In *Circles of Care: Work and Identity in Women's Lives*, edited by E. K. Abel and M. K. Nelson. 35–62. Albany: State University of New York Press.

Fried, M. 1987. "Babies and Bargaining: Working Parents Take Actions. A Manual on Bargaining for Work and Family Issues." Southeastern Massachusetts University: The Arnold M. Dubin Labor Education Center.

Fuller, B., and X. Liang. 1996. "Market Failure? Estimating Inequality in Preschool Availability." *Educational Evaluation and Policy Analysis*. 18, no. 1:31–49.

Galinsky. E. 1997. White House Conference on Child Care. October 23. <http://Clinton2.nara.gov/WH/New/Childcare/index.html>.

———. 1999. *Ask the Children: What America's Children Really Think About Working Parents*. New York: William Morrow.

Galinsky, E., C. Howes, S. Kontos, and C. Shinn. 1994. *The Study of Children in Family Child Care and Relative Care*. New York: Work and Families Institute.

Gallagher, J., R. Rooney, and S. Campbell. 2000. "Child Care Licensing Regulations and Child Care Quality in Four States." *Early Childhood Research Quarterly*. 14, no. 3:313–333.

Garey, A. I. 1995. "Constructing Motherhood on the Night Shift: 'Working Mothers' as 'Stay-at-Home' Moms." *Qualitative Sociology*. 18:414–437.

———. 1999. *Weaving Work & Motherhood*. Philadelphia: Temple University Press.

Gerber, M. 2001. Resources for Infant Educarers. <http://www.riee.org>.

Gerstel, N., and S. Gallaher. 1994. "Caring for Kith and Kin: Gender, Employment, and the Privatization of Care." *Social Problems*. 41:519–539.

Gilman, C. P. 1972 (1903). *The Home: Its Work and Influence*. Urbana: University of Illinois Press.

Glueck, S., and E. Glueck. 1951. *Unraveling Juvenile Delinquency*. Cambridge, Mass.: Harvard University Press.

Gonzalez-Mena, J. 2000. *Multicultural Issues in Child Care*. Mountain View, Calif.: Mayfield Publishing.

Haas, L. 1999. "Families and Work." In *Handbook of Marriage and the Family*. 2nd ed., edited by M. Sussman, S. Steinmetz, and G. Peterson. 571–613. New York: Plenum.

Hays, S. 1996. *The Cultural Contradictions of Motherhood*. New Haven, Conn.: Yale University Press.

Helburn, S. W., ed. 1995. *The Cost, Quality, and Child Outcomes in Child Care Centers Technical Report*. Denver: Department of Economics, Center for Research in Economic and Social Policy, University of Colorado at Denver.

Helburn, S. W., and C. Howes. 1996. "Child Care Cost and Quality." In Financing Child Care. 6 (2):62–82. Los Angeles: Center for the Future of Children, the David and Lucille Packard Foundation. <http://www.futureofchildren.org>.

Hertz, R. 1997. “A Typology of Approaches to Childcare: The Centerpiece of Organizing Family Life For Dual-Earner Couples.” *Journal of Family Issues*. 18:355–385.

Hertz, R., and F.I.T. Ferguson. 1996. “Childcare Choices and Constraints in the United States: Social Class, Race and the Influence of Family Views.” *Journal of Comparative Family Studies*. 27, no 2:249–280.

Hill Collins, P. 1994. “Shifting the Center: Race, Class, and Feminist Theorizing about Motherhood.” In *Mothering: Ideology, Experience and Agency*, edited by E. Nakano Glenn, G. Chang, and L. R. Forcey. 45–66. New York: Routledge.

Hobbs, N., P. R. Dokecki, K. V. Hoover-Dempsey, R. M. Moroney, M. W. Shayne, and K. H. Weeks. 1984. *Strengthening Families*. San Francisco: Jossey-Bass.

Hochschild, A. R. 1973. *The Unexpected Community*. Englewood Cliffs, N.J.: Prentice-Hall.

Hochschild, A. R., with A. Machung. 1989. *The Second Shift*. New York: Avon Books.

Hofferth, S. L., A. Brayfield, S. Deich, and P. Holcomb. 1991. *National Childcare Survey, 1990*. A National Association for the Education of Young Children (NAEYC) study/conducted by the Urban Institute. 91–95. Washington, D.C.: The Urban Institute Press.

Hoffman, L. W., and L. M. Youngblade. 1999. *Mothers at Work: Effects on Children's Well-Being*. Cambridge, U.K.: Cambridge University Press.

Hughes, R. 1985. “The Informal Help-Giving of Home and Center Child Care Providers.” *Family Relations*. 34:359–366.

Jacobs, F. H., and M. W. Davies, eds. 1994. *More Than Kissing Babies? Current Child and Family Policy in the United States*. Westport, Conn.: Auburn House.

Joffe, C. E. 1977. *Friendly Intruders: Childcare Professionals and Family Life*. Berkeley: University of California Press.

Kagan, S. L., with P. Neville. 1994. *Integrating Services for Children and Families*. New Haven, Conn.: Yale University Press.

Kids Count Data Book. 1998. State Profiles of Child Well-Being 1998. The Annie E. Casey Foundation. 701 St. Paul Street. Baltimore, Md. 21202. <www.necf.org>.

Kontos, S. 1984. “Congruence of Parent and Early Childhood Staff Perceptions of Parenting.” *Parenting Studies*. 1:5–10.

Kontos, S., and L. Dunn. 1989. “Attitudes of Caregivers, Maternal Experiences with Day Care, and Children's Development.” *Journal of Applied Developmental Psychology*. 10:37–51.

Kontos, S., C. Howes, M. Shinn, and E. Galinsky. 1995. *Quality in Family Child Care and Relative Care*. New York: Teachers College Press.

Kontos, S., H. Raikes, and A. Woods. 1983. “Early Childhood Staff Attitudes Toward Their Parent Clientele.” *Child Care Quarterly*. 12:45–58.

Kontos, S., and W. Wells. 1986. “Attitudes of Caregivers and the Day Care Experiences of Families.” *Early Childhood Research Quarterly*. 1:47–67.

Ladd-Taylor, M., and L. Umansky. 1998. “Introduction.” In *“Bad” Mothers: The Politics of Blame in Twentieth-Century America*, edited by M. Ladd-Taylor and L. Umansky. 1–20. New York: New York University Press.

Lajewski, H. C. 1959. “Child Care Arrangements of Full-Time Working Mothers.” Children's Bureau Publication no. 378. Washington, D.C.: Government Printing Office.

Lamb, M. E., J. Pleck, and E. Charnov. 1985. “Paternal Behavior in Humans.” *American Zoologist*. 25:883–894.

Lamphere, L., P. Zavella, and F. Gonzales, with P. B. Evans. 1993. *Sunbelt Working Mothers: Reconciling Family and Factory*. Ithaca, N.Y.: Cornell University Press.

Leslie, L. A., E. A. Anderson, and M. P. Branson. 1991. “Responsibility for Children: The Role of Gender and Employment.” *Journal of Family Issues*. 12, no. 2:197–210.

Lewis, J. 1997. “Mother's Love: The Construction of an Emotion in Nineteenth-Century America.” In *Mothers & Motherhood: Readings in American History*, edited by R. D. Apple and J. Golden. 52–71. Columbus: Ohio State University Press.

Lincoln, Y. S., and E. G. Guba. 1985. *Naturalistic Inquiry.* Newbury Park, Calif.: Sage.

Macdonald, C. 1996. “Shadow Mothers: Nannies, Au Pairs, and Invisible Work.” In *Working in the Service Sector*, edited by C. L. Macdonald and C. Sirianni. 244–263. Philadelphia: Temple University Press.

———. 1998. “Manufacturing Motherhood: The Shadow Work of Nannies and Au Pairs.” *Qualitative Sociology*. 2, no. 1:25–53.

Macdonald, C. L., and C. Sirianni. 1996. “The Service Society and Changing Experience of Work.” In *Working in the Service Sector*, edited by Cameron Lynne Macdonald and Carmen Sirianni. 1–26. Philadelphia: Temple University Press.

Machung, A. 1989. “Talking Career, Thinking Job: Gender Differences in Career and Family Expectations of Berkeley Seniors.” *Feminist Studies*. 15:35–58.

McDonnell, J. T. 1998. “On Being the“‘Bad’ Mother of an Autistic Child.” In *“Bad” Mothers: The Politics of Blame in Twentieth-Century America*, edited by M. Ladd-Taylor and L. Umansky. 220–229. New York: New York University Press.

Michel, S. 1999. *Children's Interests/Mother's Rights: The Shaping of America's Child Care Policy.* New Haven, Conn.: Yale University Press.

Murray, S. 1998. “Child Care Work: Intimacy in the Shadows of Family-Life.” *Qualitative Sociology*. 21, no. 2:149–168.

Nakano Glenn, E. 1986. *Issei, Nisei, Warbride: Three Generations of Japanese American Women in Domestic Service*. Philadelphia: Temple University Press.

Nakano Glenn, E. 1994. “Social Constructions of Mothering: A Thematic Overview.” In *Mothering: Ideology, Experience and Agency*, edited by E. Nakano Glenn, G. Chang, and L. R. Forcey. 1–32. New York: Routledge.

Nakano Glenn, E., G. Chang, and L. R. Forcey. 1994. *Mothering: Ideology, Experience and Agency.* New York: Routledge.

National Association of the Education of Young Children. 2001. <http://www.naeyc.org/accreditation/faq_3.htm>.

National Center for Early Development and Learning. 2001. <http://www.fpg.unc.edu/~NCEDL/index.htm>.

National Child Care Staffing Study. 1989. *Who Cares?: Child Care Teachers and the Quality of Care in America*. Oakland, Calif.: Child Care Employee Project.

National Institute of Child Health and Development. 1997. “The Effects of Infant Child Care on Infant-Mother Attachment Security: Results of the NICHD Study of Early Child Care.” *Child Development*. 68:860–879.

National Maternal and Child Health Resource Center on Cultural Competency. 1994. Brochure. 1100 West 49th Street, Austin, Tex.

Nelson, M. K. 1990. *Negotiated Care: The Experience of Family Day Care Providers.* Philadelphia: Temple University Press.

New, C., and M. David. 1985. *For Children's Sake. Making Childcare More Than Women's Business.* New York: Penguin Books.

Palmer, P. 1989. *Domesticity and Dirt: Housewives and Domestic Servants in the United States, 1920–1945.* Philadelphia: Temple University Press.

Pence, A. B., and H. Goelman. 1987. "Silent Partners: Parents of Children in Three Types of Day Care." *Early Childhood Research Quarterly.* 2:103–118.

Pesquera, B. 1985. "Work and Family: A Comparative Analysis of Professional, Clerical and Blue-Collar Chicana Workers." Ph.D. diss., University of California, Berkeley.

Powell, D. R. 1978a. "Correlates of Parent-teacher Communication Frequency and Diversity." *Journal of Educational Research.* 71:333–343.

———. 1978b. "The Interpersonal Relationship Between Parents and Caregivers in Day Care Settings." *American Journal of Orthopsychiatry.* 48:680–689.

———. 1989. "From the Perspective of Children: Continuity between Families and Early Childhood Programs." In *Families and Early Childhood Programs,* edited by D. Powell. 23–51. Washington D.C.: National Association for the Education of Young Children.

———. 1998. "Reweaving Parents into the Fabric of Care." *Young Children.* 53, no. 5:60–66.

Presser, H. B. 1986. "Shift Work Among American Women and Child Care." *Journal of Marriage and the Family.* 48:551–586.

———. 1989. "Some Economic Complexities of Child Care Provided by Grandmothers." *Journal of Marriage and the Family.* 51:581–591.

Quadagno, J. 1994. *The Color of Welfare.* New York: Oxford University Press.

Ritzer, G. 1993. *The McDonaldization of Society.* Thousand Oaks, Calif.: Pine Forge Press.

Rollins, J. 1985. *Between Women: Domestics and Their Employers.* Philadelphia: Temple University Press.

Romero, M. 1992. *Maid in the U.S.A.* New York: Routledge.

Rose, E. 1998. "Taking on a Mother's Job: Day Care in the 1920s and 1930s." In *"Bad" Mothers: The Politics of Blame in Twentieth-Century America,* edited by M. Ladd-Taylor and L. Umansky. 67–98. New York: New York University Press.

Rubin, J. 1997. Panelist, White House Conference on Child Care. October 23. <http://Clinton2.nara.gov/WH/New/Childcare/index.html>.

Schwartz, F. N. 1989. "Management Women and the New Facts of Life." *Harvard Business Review.* (January-February): 65–76.

Segura, D. 1994. "Working at Motherhood: Chicana and Mexicana Immigrant Mothers and Employment." In *Mothering: Ideology, Experience and Agency,* edited by E. Nakano Glenn, G. Chang, and L. R. Forcey. 211–236. New York: Routledge.

Sigel, I. E. 1987. "Does Hothousing Rob Children of Their Childhood?" *Early Childhood Research Quarterly.* 2:211–225.

Skold, K. 1988. "The Interest of Feminist and Children in Child Care." In *Feminism, Children, and the New Families,* edited by S. M. Dornbusch and M. H. Strober. New York: Guilford Press.

Small, S., and G. Eastman. 1991. "Rearing Adolescents in Contemporary Society: A Conceptual Framework for Understanding the Responsibilities and Needs of Parents." *Family Relations*. 40:455–462.

Smith, A. B., and P. M. Hubbard. 1988. "The Relationship between Parent/Staff Communication and Children's Behavior in Early Childhood Settings." *Early Childhood Development and Care*. 35:13–28.

Snarey, J. 1993. *How Fathers Care for the Next Generation*. Cambridge, Mass.: Harvard University Press.

Steinberg, L. D., and C. Green. 1979. "What Parents Seek in Day Care." *Human Ecology Forum*. Fall: 13–40.

Steinfels, M. O. 1973. *Who's Minding the Children: The History and Politics of Day Care in America*. New York: Simon and Schuster.

Stockinger, J. 2000. Personal statement delivered at Work and Family: Expanding the Horizons conference. San Francisco.

Sweeney, John. 1997. White House Conference on Child Care. October 23. <http://Clinton2.nara.gov/WH/New/Childcare/index.html>.

Thorne, B., with M. Yalom. 1982. *Rethinking the Family*. New York: Longman.

Tice, K. 1998. "Mending Rosa's 'Working Ways': A Case Study of an African American Mother and Breadwinner." In *"Bad Mothers": The Politics of Blame in Twentieth-Century America,* edited by M. Ladd-Taylor and L. Umansky. 31–40. New York: New York University Press.

Tuominen, M. 1991. "Caring for Profit: The Social, Economic, and Political Significance of For-profit Child Care." *Social Service Review*. September: 450–467.

———. 1994. "The Hidden Organization of Labor: Gender, Race/Ethnicty and Childcare Work in the Formal and Informal Economy." *Sociological Perspectives*. 37:229–245.

———. 1997. "Exploitation or Opportunity? The Contradictions of Child-Care Policy in the Contemporary United States." *Women & Politics*.18, no. 1:53–80.

———. 1998. "Motherhood and the Market: Mothering and Employment Opportunities Among Mexicana, African American, and Euro-American Family Day Care Workers." *Sociological Focus*. 31, no. 1:59–77.

Tuttle, R. C. 1994. "Determinants of Father's Participation in Child Care." *International Journal of Sociology of the Family*. 24:113–125.

U.S. Bureau of Labor Statistics. 1987. "Over half of mothers with children one year old or under in labor force in March 1987." Press release. USDL 87–3345. 769. P. Washington, D.C.: Government Printing Office. June 16.

———. 1997. "Unemployment Characteristics of Families: 1996." August 12. <http://www.bls.census.gov/cps/pub/famee_0697.htm>.

U.S. Department of Labor. Women's Bureau. 1997. "Child Care Workers: Facts on Working Women." No. 98–1, November. <http://www.dol.gov/dol/wb/public/wb_pubs/childc.htm>.

———. 1999. "Work Related Child Care Statistics." <http://www.dol.gov/dol/wb/childcare/ccstats.htm>.

———. 2000. "20 Facts on Women Workers." March. <http://www.dol.gov/dol/wb/public/wb_pubs/20fact00.htm>.

Uttal, L. 1996a. "Custodial Care, Surrogate Care, and Coordinated Care: Employed Mothers and the Meaning of Child Care." *Gender & Society.* 10:291–311.

———. 1996b. "Racial Safety and Cultural Maintenance: The Childcare Concerns of Women of Color." *Ethnic Studies Review.* 19, no. 1: 43–59.

———. 1997. "'Trust Your Instincts': Racial Ethnic and Class-Based Preferences in Employed Mothers' Childcare Choices." *Qualitative Sociology.* 20, no. 2:253–274.

Uttal, L., and M. Tuominen. 1999. "Tenuous Relationships: Exploitation, Emotion, and Racial Ethnic Significance in Paid Childcare Work." *Gender & Society.* 13, no. 6:755–777

Werner, E. E. 1984. *Child Care: Kith, Kin, and Hired Hands.* Baltimore, Md.: University Park Press.

Willer, B., S. L. Hofferth, E. E. Kisker, E. Divine-Hawkins, E. Farquar, and F. B. Glantz. 1991. *The Demand and Supply of Child Care in 1990.* Washington, D.C.: National Association for the Education of Young Children.

Wrigley, J. 1987. "The Implications of a Class Divide: Professionally-Employed Mothers and Their Children's Day Care Providers." Paper presented at the annual meeting of the American Educational Research Association, Washington, D.C.

———. 1989. "Different Care for Different Kids: Social Class and Child Care Policy." *Educational Policy.* 3:421–439.

———. 1990. "Children's Caregivers and Ideologies of Parental Inadequacy." In *Circles of Care: Work and Identity in Women's Lives,* edited by E. K. Abel and M. K. Nelson. 290–312. Albany: State University of New York Press.

———. 1995. *Other People's Children.* New York: Basic Books.

Youcha, G. 1995. *Minding the Children.* New York: Scribner.

Zavella, P. 1987. *Women's Work & Chicano Families: Cannery Workers of the Santa Clara Valley.* Ithaca, N.Y.: Cornell University Press.

Zigler, E., and P. Turner. 1982. "Parents and Day Care Workers: A Failed Partnership?" In *Day Care Scientific and Social Policy Issues,* edited by E. Zigler and E. Gordon. 174–182. Boston: Auburn House Press.

Zinsser, C. 1991. *Raised in East Urban: Child Care Changes in a Working Class Community.* New York: Teachers College Press.

Index

About the Author

Lynet Uttal likes to ask "What is going on here?" about matters that are important to creating a more humane society and caring relationships. She is a sociologist working in the Human Development and Family Studies department at the University of Wisconsin, Madison, and regularly teaches "Racial Ethnic Families" and "Qualitative Methods."